A History of Adoption in England and Wales 1850–1961

This book is dedicated to

Mrs E.P. Taylor
to honour her boundless courage in
overwhelming circumstances
and to celebrate her infinite love for her twins.

A History of
Adoption in
England and Wales
1850–1961

GILL ROSSINI

Pen & Sword
FAMILY HISTORY

First published in Great Britain in 2014 by
PEN AND SWORD FAMILY HISTORY
an imprint of
Pen and Sword Books Ltd
47 Church Street
Barnsley
South Yorkshire S70 2AS

ISBN 978 1 78159 395 0

Printed and bound in England
by CPI Group (UK) Ltd, Croydon, CR0 4YY

Typeset in Times New Roman by
CHIC GRAPHICS

Pen & Sword Books Ltd incorporates the imprints of Pen & Sword
Archaeology, Atlas, Aviation, Battleground, Discovery,
Family History, History, Maritime, Military, Naval, Politics, Railways,
Select, Social History, Transport, True Crime, and Claymore Press,
Frontline Books, Leo Cooper, Praetorian Press, Remember When,
Seaforth Publishing and Wharncliffe.

For a complete list of Pen and Sword titles please contact
Pen and Sword Books Limited
47 Church Street, Barnsley, South Yorkshire, S70 2AS, England
E-mail: enquiries@pen-and-sword.co.uk
Website: www.pen-and-sword.co.uk

Contents

Acknowledgements

My grateful thanks go firstly to Pen and Sword's History Imprint editor Jennifer Newby, whose patient, good natured and wise guidance has been beyond value as this book has progressed, and who has put up with my endless questions over its illustrations with immense good humour. Also a huge thank you to Amanda Kay for her patient and highly professional editorial guidance, without which this book would have been the poorer.

The grant given to me by the Authors' Foundation has been a boon in helping me to purchase materials necessary for my research; my grateful thanks to them.

Thank you to all the staff in archive departments and libraries who have helped identify sources for the history of adoption. I have the utmost respect and gratitude for your professional guidance.

I have had the ultimate sounding board for my ideas and theories – the many hundreds of family history students who have endured my teaching over more than 20 years, but in particular, the students from North and Mid Wales and Greater Manchester, who over the past seven years, have been my lively, intelligent and completely constructive collective muse. You have been more valuable than I can say. Special thanks go to Viv, Ruth, Gaynor, Marianna and Pam for their kindly interest and practical support.

To my darling partner Gill, my everlasting gratitude and love for tolerating the piles of paper, files, books, monologues and ponderings generated by this project, and for sharing your own experiences with me.

Finally, my deepest respect and love to Mum and her twins, for all they have gone through, and for sharing it with me. Thank you for giving me the gift of your stories.

A Note Regarding
Confidentiality

A need for confidentiality – even secrecy – has always been present when it comes to adoption until very recently, and even now it is an issue that must be taken into account. This book is no exception in respecting that need. In stories recounted by living persons or in which living persons are mentioned, all names and locations have been changed to respect and protect the individuals concerned.

A Note Regarding
Terminology

Apart from those with a single interest in adoption and its history, it is sincerely hoped that this book will appeal to a wide range of readers – family, social and local historians, of course, but also those with an interest in the history of childhood, child educators, and students of child development. I have tried not to assume any prior in-depth knowledge of the terminology or chronology of this period, especially regarding the issues surrounding the welfare of children. To help clarify what the narrative has not made evident, I have added a glossary of the key terms used in the text.

Illustrations

1. Abandoned baby, taken from *The Pictorial Times*, 1846. Author's own collection.
2. Fallen woman being saved, taken from a vintage magic lantern slide used to promote the work of an East London mission; approximately 1900. Author's own collection.
3. Queen Victoria and her children, an illustration from the *Illustrated London News*, 12 July 1856, depicting the Queen and her children attending the opening of Wellington College. Author's own collection.
4. Croydon Asylum for Fatherless Children (later known as Reedham Orphanage), Reedham, 1894. Author's own collection.
5. Girls at the Reedham Orphanage, Surrey, working in the ironing room. An illustration from the *Illustrated London News*, 14 July 1894. Author's own collection.
6. Dr Barnardo's Village Homes for Girls, Barkingside. Vintage postcard, publisher/printer unknown. Approximately 1910. Author's own collection.
7. Postcard published by Bamforth and Co, approximately 1915–20. Part of a set of 'Song Cards' with each image illustrating a verse from a popular song. Author's own collection.
8. Advertisement, c. 1920, from *Doidge's Western Counties Illustrated Annual*. Printed by Hoyton and Cole, Plymouth. Author's own collection.
9. Advertisement for the Waifs and Strays Society, using its connection with the Duke of Kent and his new wife, Princess Marina, to raise its profile and encourage donations. The Duke and Princess married on 29 November 1934. Publication unknown. Author's own collection.
10. The Duke and Duchess of York and their daughters Elizabeth and Margaret Rose. From an informal photograph, 1937. Photographer not known. Author's own collection.
11. 'Playing the Field'. Comic postcard by E.T.W. Dennis and Sons Ltd, Scarborough. 1939–45. Author's own collection.

12. Advertisement from *Punch* magazine, 23 April 1924, for Almata, an artificial baby milk. Author's own collection.
13. Postcard sent by the Church of England Children's Society (formerly Waifs and Strays), used as a thank you note in response to a donation. Postmarked 8 January 1955. Author's own collection.
14. Front cover of the booklet, *A Baby is Adopted: The Children's Society's Adoption Book*, by Margaret Kornitzer and published by The Church of England Children's Society, London, 1950. Author's own collection.

CHAPTER 1

Introduction and Background

Adoption is one of the most emotive subjects in social history, and in family history in particular. Express an interest in adoption – especially those in past generations – and the majority of family historians have an adoption story to tell you about from their own genealogies.

Adoption is only one event in a person's life, and yet it can resonate not only throughout that person's life, but right through a family history too. One of the reasons it is such a compelling subject is perhaps its inherent and sometimes frustrating mystery. England and Wales were late in legislating for formal adoptions compared to other countries. Before that point there was a vast confusion of makeshift solutions to the perennial problem of the unwanted child or baby, especially those born out of wedlock.

The shame of being an unmarried mother, or of having a single mother in the family, led to a bewildering number of ways for dealing with these 'misfits', many of which involved the family closing ranks, dealing with the matter secretly, and never talking about it again. However, families being what they are, eventually someone usually breaks ranks and an ill-chosen, disingenuous or malicious remark could blow the cover of a secret that has been kept close for generations. All family historians love intrigue of this kind, but the problems of solving the adoption mysteries in a family tree can seem insurmountable. Even after 1926 – the year adoptions were legally formalised in England and Wales – the official secrecy around an adoption deters most enquirers who are not the adoptee themselves from tackling the research.

What Exactly is Adoption?
In order to explore this topic, a definition of adoption must be arrived at, but this is not as simple as it first appears. In the twenty-first century, we tend to think of adoption in a narrow sense, as the taking into one's

family through a legal procedure, the child of another person or family. It is a very small definition for an event of life-changing and highly emotional significance. The definition can be widened. For example, it could be said that whenever a person or an organisation is *in loco parentis* for any length of time, they are in an adoptive situation, or at the very least, are foster parents. This would then widen the definition to include the carers of evacuee children in World War Two, as well as the poor relief authorities caring for children in the nineteenth century and early twentieth century.

If one accepts organisations as adopters, children's homes and orphanages must then be added. The definition of adoption would also apply to family members who informally took on a relative's child, although they would be unlikely to see this as adoption, more as helping out the parent concerned out of familial loyalty. In 1937, the Horsbrugh Committee Report (see Chapter 4) described adoption as follows:

> *The essence of an adoption, whether legalised or de facto, seems to us to lie in the creation of an artificial family relationship analogous to that of parent and child ... which is accepted by all parties as permanent. The child is absorbed into the family of the adopter and is treated as if it were their own natural child.*

There is a word of warning to be borne in mind with regard to this statement, for not all natural children are treated with love, nurtured, and guided as they should be. Adoption does not always have a happy ending because the lives of children are variable whatever their beginnings, and it includes the whole spectrum of stories, just like those from any other walk of life.

Why Adopt?
What were/are the reasons for adoption? For decades, adoption has largely been seen from just a few perspectives. Today, it is a major option for couples who for whatever reason – infertility or previous illness, for example – are not able to have biological children of their own. It is seen as a form of altruism or humanistic action, to take in as your own the unwanted children of another person – often those with disabilities or perhaps those from another country altogether. Such adopters may feel they are 'rescuing' children from this group.

12

INTRODUCTION AND BACKGROUND

Some people have mixed families, with biological children, stepchildren and adopted children together; others may have taken on the children of a deceased, homeless or less abled relative. Over a hundred years ago, or even less, other reasons for adoption can be added to the list, although that is not to say that they are not considered as reasons by some people today. For example, adoption was used to create heirs for property, and to stop a family line dying out, particularly important for a family affluent enough to have substantial financial or property interests.

Altruism also had a place in the past in that some people would take on a child from an orphanage or children's home in order to give her/him a family. It was also a loose term for the disposal of an illegitimate baby or small child to a baby farmer (see Chapter 2), the 'industry' that gave adoption such a bad name in the nineteenth century and which sadly persisted into the twentieth century, although of course some unwanted babies must have been sold to what turned out to be doting and excellent parents. In the past, adopted children could be taken on to look after their parents in old age, or to work for the family, which led to some distressing cases of cruelty, even after the 1926 Adoption of Children Act. Older children were particularly vulnerable to this form of abuse.

Adoption has for millennia been seen as a solution to housing an unwanted, abandoned (a 'foundling') or orphaned child. Victorians must have taken comfort from passages and stories which highlight adoption in the Hebrew and Christian Bibles – in the Book of Esther, the child Esther is orphaned when her parents die, and she is adopted and raised by her older cousin Mordecai. Esther is an adoption success story, as she goes on to become the consort of King Xerxes. Moses as a baby is also an adoptee – found alone in the reeds at the edge of a river, he becomes the beloved adopted child of the Pharoah's daughter and of course as an adult, after many tribulations, he becomes the saviour of the Jewish people.

These and various other allusions to the concept of adoption reinforce the notion of adoption as a morally and culturally legitimate act. There are Classical allusions to adoption too – in the law of Ancient Rome, the paterfamilias or male head of the household had the right to give up a child for adoption by another family. Usually, it was the oldest boy who had a good health record and some education; in fact, girls could not be adopted and women could not adopt a child in their own right. Classically

13

educated men in the nineteenth and twentieth centuries would have been well aware of this completely open Roman system, which was entirely pragmatic and seen as a normal thing to do.

A Word About Illegitimacy

It is virtually impossible to write about the history of adoption without addressing the topic of illegitimacy because the vast majority of babies and children who were adopted were born outside of a marriage – either the mother was not married at all, being single or a widow, or the mother was married, but her husband was not the father of the child. Only a small proportion of children who were 'candidates' for adoption were available because of the death of a married parent. Consequently, considerable attention is paid to the situation of the illegitimate child in this study, and their birth families.

How Easy is Adoption to Research?

Bearing in mind that adoptions of all kinds in the period covered by this book – both informal and legal – are restricted by secrecy, or just plain issues of confidentiality, it is hardly surprising that many people think that researching the history of adoption is well nigh impossible. However, given that the definition of adoption needs to be viewed in a broad sense for much of the period covered, we can readily gain a picture of what was happening to many adopted, abandoned or unwanted children and their carers, even though the adoption files may be closed. Many children and their mothers were, in a sense, 'hidden in plain sight', in that everyone in the community knew they were there but chose to ignore them or treat them with veiled hostility.

The huge growth in family history has uncovered many stories of informal adoptions via census returns and the discovery of family papers, and as time goes by, more papers uncovering the history of orphanages, adoption societies and children's charities have been released for the perusal of historians. Historians are also fortunate that the period covered by this book saw a huge upsurge, not only in literacy but in popular publications such as provincial newspapers, women's magazines and fiction – photographs abound too, and there was great activity within social action groups such as children's charities. Other records may include court records, census returns, oral history sources, police records, trade directories and legal papers such as private agreements.

INTRODUCTION AND BACKGROUND

The secret is to approach the story of these families, children and the agencies who tried to help them, with a broad sweep. To look too closely at the plain facts of the story of the drive towards legislation is to miss the human aspects of the tale, and to lose touch with the people who were the subjects of all this attention. These people can be split into three groups: the children themselves; their birth mothers and other birth family; and the agencies, individuals or families who took the children into their institutions, homes and families.

These are the building blocks of the story of adoption. Attention is also given to the wider context in which this story is set – unless one understands how the nature of family was seen as at a given time, it will be more difficult to appreciate how adoption fits in to the whole. The final section of the book offers some practical advice and comprehensive lists for researching the subject at various different times from 1850 to 1961.

What Was Happening Before 1850?

To be born out of wedlock was a huge stigma. William Blackstone's *Laws of England*, written in the middle of the eighteenth century, refers to a bastard or 'spurious' child as '*Filius populi*' – child of the people: 'The rights [*of the bastard child*] are very few, being only such as he can acquire; for he can inherit nothing, being looked upon as the son of nobody, and sometimes called filius nullius [*son of no one*], sometimes filius populi [*son of the people*]. Yet he may gain a surname by reputation, though he has none by inheritance.' Therefore, in general terms, a *filius populi*, if he/she belonged to the people in a loose sense, could not have ancestors and looking forward, could not inherit from anyone either, as they had no true place in a legitimate family. The child had no status, and no connections.

Furthermore, *filius populi* was the product of bad blood, and as such, would be nothing but trouble. Coming from a mother of low morals (the father of the child was rarely labelled in this way), it was assumed that the child would be morally unsound, and worse still, would be a burden on the authorities, in particular the Poor Relief system. It was very much a case of the sins of the female parent being visited upon the child. This mindset was to continue more or less unchanged well into the latter half of the twentieth century.

The following poem, by Helen Leigh, the wife of a Cheshire curate, was written in 1788:

15

A HISTORY OF ADOPTION

'The Natural Child'
Let not the title of my verse offend,
Nor let the pride contract her rigid brow;
That helpless Innocence demands a friend,
Virtue herself will cheerfully allow:

And should my pencil prove too weak to paint,
The ills attendant on the babe ere born;
Whose parents swerved from virtue's mild restraint,
Forgive the attempt, nor treat the Muse with scorn.

Yon rural farm, where Mirth was wont to dwell,
Of Melancholy, now appears the seat;
Solemn and silent as the hermit's cell —
Say what, my muse, has caused a change so great?

This hapless morn, an infant first saw light,
Whose innocence a better fate might claim,
Than to be shunned as hateful to the sight,
And banished soon as it receives a name.

No joy attends its entrance into life,
No smile upon its mother's face appears,
She cannot smile, alas! she is no wife;
But vents the sorrow of her heart in tears.

No father flies to clasp it to his breast,
And bless the power that gave it to his arms;
To see his form, in miniature expressed,
Or trace, with ecstasy, its mother's charms.

Unhappy babe! thy father is thy foe!
Oft shall he wish thee numbered with the dead;
His crime entails on thee a load of woe,
And sorrow heaps on thy devoted head.

INTRODUCTION AND BACKGROUND

Torn from its breast, by shame or pride,
No matter which — to hireling hands assigned;
A parent's tenderness, when thus denied,
Can it be thought its nurse is over-kind?

Too many, like this infant may we see,
Exposed, abandoned, helpless and forlorn;
Till death, misfortune's friend, has set them free,
From a rude world, which gave them nought but scorn.

Too many mothers — horrid to relate!
Soon as their infants breathe the vital air,
Deaf to their plaintive cries, their helpless state,
Led on by shame, and driven by despair,

Fell murderers to become — Here cease, my pen,
And leave these wretched victims of despair;
But oh! what punishments await the men,
Who in such depths of misery plunge the fair.

Mrs Leigh seems to have written a number of observational poems based on what she saw around her, and almost certainly wrote this poem having witnessed various illegitimate children being born in her husband's parish, with all the attendant anguish, troubles and upset.

Like many pieces of writing on the subject of bastard children, this poem has an agenda in that it tries to draw attention to the miserable plight of mother and child, rather than condemn the woman for immorality. It is full of highly emotive words and turns of phrase – 'melancholy', 'shunned', 'hateful', 'sorrow', 'shame' and 'despair' are just a selection. The message is that from birth, the child of the unwed mother is a pariah, banished not only from polite society but worse still, from all respectable society – and ignored and abandoned by the father, the very person who could secure her or his future.

Finally we have the image of the abandoned or exposed child – and the poet makes the point that too many of these sorry children are born, and therefore too many desperate mothers resort to infanticide by exposure – 'Led on by shame, and driven by despair'. One is tempted to

17

see a touch of early feminism in the final two lines as Mrs Leigh asks what punishments will be given to the men who put these fair women in this appalling condition? The answer was, of course, very little. Nearly half a century after this poem was published, the image of the desperate lone mother abandoning her baby on the desolate fells appeared in *The Pictorial Times* of 1846 (see Plate 1), suggesting that not only had the situation not improved for unmarried mothers, but that it still attracted the same level of voyeuristic disapproval as in the previous century.

Revd Thomas Robert Malthus, who wrote the influential *Essay on the Principle of Population* in 1798, had reinforced the idea that the woman should take a greater share of the blame than a man for bringing an illegitimate baby into the world, on the grounds that as the woman had no resources to care for the child or children, her offence was more conspicuous, and therefore the inconvenience to society was greater. Also, the mother was unlikely to be wrongly identified, whereas the father may well be. Not everybody saw this inequity as necessarily wholesome. The Whig politician Lord Brougham wrote:

> *Would any man hesitate to say, that if he saw his daughter in a house of ill-fame he would not hold her in a very different light from that in which he would regard his son if he discovered him in the same situation? Everybody knew that unmarried men did not lead a life of contingency, and that one-twentieth part of crimes of this description committed by a man would be the utter ruin of a female.*

Money brings power; any woman who had a child out of wedlock, and who could support herself and the baby without having to defer to or rely upon anyone else, could do as she wished. Very few women in history have been in this lucky position, and many single mothers had to turn to the parish or poor relief authorities for help and support.

Prior to the Poor Law Amendment Act of 1834, the mothers of bastard children had some security in that the putative father of the child was held to be responsible for the maintenance of the child, and after the bastardy proceedings (the legal process whereby an alleged father of an illegitimate child could be compelled to pay for his/her maintenance) had been completed, he could be arrested and imprisoned if he failed to do this.

INTRODUCTION AND BACKGROUND

At the Cornwall Quarter Sessions (roughly the equivalent of a modern magistrate's court) in the spring of 1811, James Nicholas was returned to prison for 'want of sureties to indemnify the parish of Sennen, in a case of bastardy' – in other words he had reneged on his agreement (by not having a reliable person to act as guarantor for him) and lost his freedom as a result. James would have been put under this obligation as an affiliation order would have been made against him and in favour of the mother of his illegitimate child. It compelled him to make maintenance payments to the child, of course via a third party, such as the mother or whoever was responsible for bringing the child up.

Interestingly, at the same hearing a woman named Mary Lukey appeared, having first done so in 1809 'for refusing to declare the father of her bastard child, born in the parish of Breage'. The *Royal Cornwall Gazette* reported that 'She had subsisted on the county allowance of bread and water, rather than expose the father; and still persisting in keeping the secret, she was remanded again to prison.' The *Gazette*'s correspondent wryly commented, 'Had this heroine been but half as inflexible before her faux pas, as she had been since, she had still been a vestal (a virgin).'

There is an intriguing case of history repeating itself too, as in 1826, a Sarah Williams was also placed in custody because she also refused to divulge the identity of the father of her bastard child, again chargeable to the parish of Breage. Here we have the two sides of the story; there was the obligation of the father to chip in and support his child, but on the other hand, there was an obligation on the part of the mother to reveal the identity of the father. This was primarily an issue of economics: if the mother and her baby turned to the parish for support via poor relief, the pressure was then on the Poor Law officers, usually known as Overseers, to find the father so that he could pay for mother and child's upkeep, rather than them.

However, there was growing discontent with this system, and some of the discontent was on the surface from a moral and financial point of view. On 23 May 1826, *The Times* newspaper reported on the amount of money the city of Manchester had to spend on the upkeep of illegitimate children:

> *There is every reason to believe that all the respectable factories take great pains to enforce and preserve moral discipline among*

19

the numerous classes of both sexes in their employment; but, that a great laxity of morals still prevails among the youth engaged in manufacturing industry, and more particularly among the younger, so early as fifteen or sixteen years of age ... This is a frightful evil, and the strongest discipline ought to be applied to its correction. The returns for the year just ended (for central Manchester), of mothers of illegitimate children, is 4,943.

When the 1834 Poor Law Amendment Act came into force, it included a controversial measure which made the mother the sole 'guardian' of her child until it reached the age of 16. There was a belief among those who shaped the Poor Laws that it was time that single mothers took such sole responsibility. If this was impressed upon them, would they refrain from making the same mistake again and, in the long term, birth rates of illegitimate children would fall (which over the coming years they were to claim had happened). After 1834, the intimidating process of having to prove 'in some material particular' the paternity of the child would prove impossible for most women – how in the 1830s could a woman conclusively prove that a certain man was her child's father?

In addition, bastardy proceedings could now only be initiated by the Overseers of the Poor or the Poor Law Guardians and were held at the Quarter Sessions Court. This new tightening up of the manner in which a single mother could claim redress was designed to deter her from asking for help and as a result, most mothers of illegitimate children became solely responsible for the raising of their child until he/she reached the age of 16. If the single mother could not raise her child unaided and turned to the Poor Relief authorities for help, she would have to go into the workhouse.

After 1834, workhouses had become the famously grim institutions described so evocatively by Charles Dickens, and known colloquially as 'bastilles' after the notorious Paris prison. Their raison d'être was deterrent – to make life in the workhouse so unpleasant and distanced from ordinary life that one would only go in there as a matter of life and death. Spouses were separated on entry, belongings and clothes confiscated and uniforms issued, and older children rarely saw their parents. Jobs such as oakum picking and sorting, and crushing animal bones were compulsory.

INTRODUCTION AND BACKGROUND

It is little wonder that the Victorian workhouse struck fear into the heart of the poor, and perhaps even more so with the fallen woman, who faced not only a harsh regime, but the moral disapproval of inmates and staff alike. The Board of Guardians was now empowered to 'help' the mother find the father of her child and make him responsible for its upkeep by applying to the Quarter Sessions Courts for an affiliation order, but it is highly unlikely that it was out of altruistic motives, more likely an attempt to find someone to pay for the child's upkeep other than the Poor Relief system and its beleaguered ratepayers.

This was a highly unpopular measure and led to heated debates on the subject of the single mother and what methods should be used to find her some support. After ten years of public pressure, the Poor Law Amendment Act of 1844 came into force. Now, a mother of an illegitimate child could again apply directly to the local magistrates for an affiliation order against the father, regardless of whether she was in receipt of poor relief or not.

Subject to corroborative evidence of paternity, the mother could expect to be awarded a court order promising her 10 shillings for the attendance of the midwife and 2s 6d a week until the child was 13 years old. It would be encouraging to think that the change in the law was to make it easier for the mother to seek redress against the father of her child, but as with the 1834 Act, it was more to do with other poor relief issues than concern for her welfare. In addition, fewer working-class women were likely to take this legal course of action on their own, even if they knew about the option in the first place.

On occasion, the records reveal a similarly disapproving tone directed at the fathers of illegitimate children. In August 1835, not long after the passing of the 1834 Act, an elderly chimney sweep who had fathered 21 illegitimate children became unable to do his work and applied to enter the Bishopsgate Workhouse in London. Unfortunately, even though he was no longer able to work as a chimney sweep, and his large brood of children had always been supported by his female partner and himself, he was refused admission to the workhouse by the poor relief officers – as the man said, 'The damned new Poor Law' was the cause of the hardness of heart in the parish.

Mr Brown, the Overseer of the Poor, suggested that if the poor relief officers were to take in a person of such a character, it would be injurious to the hard working members of the community, and he could not imagine having to take in a man such as this. However, at the hearing presided over by the Lord Mayor, His Lordship commanded the Overseers to allow the man to take his place in the workhouse, and criticised the new law for allowing the officers ingenious ways to withhold help from those who had not even a morsel of food to eat. However, the real reason this man was originally excluded is clearly because of his 21 illegitimate children and the hostile reaction to his common-law marriage.

CHAPTER 2

"Our Innocence is all a Sham"
Fallen Women, Displaced Children
and Public Sensibilities, 1850–1918

Children In England and Wales in the 1850s

What was it like to be a child in England and Wales at this time? The census report for 1851 stated that 'The English population contains an excessive amount of children and young people'. The population was gradually increasing across the nineteenth century: in 1851 the total population for England and Wales was 17.9 million, rising to 36.1 million by 1911.

An interesting distinction is drawn in the 1851 census report between the genealogical definition of family with its emphasis on pedigree, and what the census statisticians regarded as a family unit: 'The first, most intimate, and perhaps most important community, is the FAMILY, not considered as the children of one parent, but as the persons under one head'. In other words, any group of people living together under one roof and sharing a table were to be regarded as a family, and the head of the household/family or 'occupier' was the person responsible for paying the rent for a whole or part of a property. This would also mean that a single person living alone would be regarded as a family or household.

Taking this definition, the number of families in England and Wales in 1851 was 3,712,290, an increase of nearly 2 million since the first census was taken in 1801. The average 'family' comprised five persons – usually a male and female partnership, married or otherwise, and their children, plus servants, lodgers or extended family. The average age of marriage was 26 years for women and 28 years for men, but boys of 14 and girls of 12 could consent to marry, with parental consent needed until 21, the age of majority. If this very fluid definition of family was reflected by the population on a practical level, then it would overturn many of our preconceptions of what Victorians thought of as a family unit, and leave the concept of the 'family' wide open to the addition of children who were not genetically connected to the key members of the household.

There was nothing sentimental about the way in which the children of labouring families were treated during this period. Children often drank alcohol, so the dosing of babies with opiate-based sedatives seemed perfectly normal in comparison – however, there is evidence that not all parents were aware of the opiate content of the sedatives, but were just happy that it afforded them some peace.

Children were also treated like adults in the eyes of the law, and punished accordingly. Later in the century, the Stockport Town Thieves Book, a ledger kept by local police to identify regular miscreants, featured 12-year-old petty thieves alongside habitual, long-standing and mature adult offenders.

From today's perspective, it is shocking to think that 160 years ago, children were not always emotionally valuable; they were a commodity, to be moved around, bartered with, sold, and passed on at will. The theft of children – the word theft is chosen advisedly, as abduction would suggest an acknowledgement that children had a freedom that could be curtailed by kidnapping – was undertaken because they could be sold on to beggars (as a useful 'prop' to tug at the public's heart strings), or their clothes taken and sold on into the profitable second-hand clothes market. They could be sold to unscrupulous employers such as chimney sweeps or pushed into prostitution.

Those who stole children could, of course, also exploit the vulnerable childless couple by offering to sell them a child to 'adopt'. Sometimes, it was the parents who sold the child into any one of these situations. In other cases, the child became a source of profit for the lawless to exploit. Yet, at the same time, children were given responsibilities that would only be undertaken by adults today – care of babies and young children, often in the complete absence of any responsible adults; tasks in industrial and agricultural work that involved dangerous tools and machinery; and heavy work at home.

Children were expected to pull their weight in a family in whatever way they were needed, and because of what they had heard and learned, they feared the possibility of ending up in the workhouse as much as their parents did. The notion of what defined a child was completely different in the nineteenth century, and over-sentimentalised images of cherubic children in pretty clothes from more affluent families sat awkwardly with images of ragged street children in Victorian culture. A child was a small human whom you could own, exploit, love and abuse as you wished, and then discard at will.

It would be all too easy to condemn society and its citizens in the mid nineteenth century because they had such wildly different views about children to the average adult of today. One must guard against this, however. Children were valued, but in a very different way, and the parent who sent a child out to work at a very young age, or insisted she or he stayed at home to learn skills, no doubt truly believed that to provide some security for oneself in those days would be much more important than anything else, including an education.

With security came respectability, a modicum of status, and the hope of marrying better than someone from a pauper background could aspire to. The one day of the week when many children received a form of education would be attending Sunday school, that is, if they could be spared from their chores.

The Victorian Child: Statistics from the 1851 Census for England and Wales and Elsewhere

In 1851 9,985,133 persons were legally classified as 'infants', that is, under the age of 21 years.
Included in this figure are:
• 578,743 babies aged 0 to one year
• 2,156,456 children aged one year to five years
• 2,456,066 children between the ages of five and ten years
• 2,256,815 children between the ages of ten and fifteen years.

In England and Wales in 1851, the number of registered live births was 615,865.
• Of these 615,865 births, 42,000 were born outside marriage.
• For every 1,000 babies born in 1851, only 522 reached the age of five years.
• There were 1,509,520 children – 'orphans' – living with a sole widowed parent.
• 1,467,185 'natural' families had no children.
• Half of all children in England and Wales aged five to fifteen years – 2,347,291 – were receiving no formal education.
• 705,409 children aged five to fifteen years had employment outside the home; 1,583,732 children in the same age group were 'employed' within the home.

25

Despite legislation in the 1830s and 1840s for factory and mine workers to restrict the roles in which and length of time children would work in those environments, it is startling how many children were still toiling for long hours as employees. The number of boys aged from five to ten years who worked in the textile industry in 1851 was 4,434, with 1,209 children in this age range still working in the coal mining industry. Well over half a million people were classified as domestic servants in 1851, and this would include a substantial number of those whom the twenty-first century citizen would regard as young children, working very long hours and doing arduous manual labour.

As can be seen, many children never went to school at all, and worked from being very small, either at home or in a workplace. For many struggling parents in labouring families, to send a child to school would be to devalue her or him as a personal, family and economic asset. The lives of children displaced from family, work or community could be even worse.

The 'Displaced Children' of Victorian England and Wales

How would one define the 'displaced child' of Victorian England and Wales? It could be said that such a child is any minor who was not closely connected to, and benefiting from, one family unit as a means of support. The reasons for this detachment varied.

As mentioned above, many children had to work and this left them vulnerable to physical, psychological and developmental damage. Some children in adult environments suffered sexual abuse. Children who became the responsibility of the Poor Law system might find themselves in a workhouse, or later on be boarded out with a family they did not know, or as older children, may be placed in an institution – sooner rather than later, if they had a disability and were not seen as having any economic worth. Other pauper children were placed in apprenticeships and could be moved considerable distances from home as pauper employees, thereby isolating them from extended family. Children, some as young as 12 or even less, who went into domestic service – either in a household or on a farm – were equally isolated and invariably at the bottom of the staff hierarchy too.

However, these children were part of a system in which someone was supposed to have responsibility for them. There were thousands of children who had no one to watch over them at all, who lived on the streets and survived as best they could. There were many reasons why children ended up as 'Street Arabs', as they were known. Some babies and young children were simply abandoned, while others had a family who relied on their petty thieving, odd jobs or prostitution to survive and therefore had a vested interest in the child living on the street. Some had run away from abusive or desperately poor backgrounds, while yet others had travelled to an urban area in search of work, but found none.

These children slept where they could, ate when they could, and had even fewer opportunities for health care, nurturing or education than the average poor child with a family. Later in the Victorian era, they were to be the primary target for child welfare groups such as the Waifs and Strays Society, who strove to rebuild the lives of these forgotten children.

Another major group of displaced children were those separated from the nuclear family unit by bereavement. Orphans may have been farmed out to any relative who had the space and resources to take them in, and little consideration would have been given to the process of grieving – such sentiment was reserved for those with the economic leisure to indulge.

However, the group most likely to be displaced in one way or another, was the illegitimate child. Their position in the wider family may well have been precarious, partly because of innate hostility towards the child (the focus of blame for the embarrassment often fell on the child) and could sometimes lead to them being moved from one family group to the other as they grew up. Failing that, such children often grew up with grandparents and did not get to know their mother well, or at all.

This displacement, or isolation from the relatives who under different circumstances may have had the strongest bond with them, made these children much more vulnerable to all manner of negative experiences, and more likely to be in need of the assistance of external sources of help. One piece of legislation that would have provided a framework of stability for children without a stable home or family life was legal adoption. In America, adoption legislation began in 1851, but in England and Wales, a new century would have to dawn before legal adoption was even seriously considered and publicly debated.

In the meantime, the overall picture of child care, especially for children without a family to call their own, remained precarious and often chaotic. However, there were not even many charitable institutions dedicated to the care of children at this point, and certainly not enough to deal with the thousands of vulnerable children; all this was yet to come. For the time being, children remained valuable commodities, useful economic units, and entirely dispensable.

There is one group of displaced children whom it will be almost impossible to trace, at least until they are adults and able to make their own decisions to take their place in society. There is anecdotal evidence that large numbers of illegitimate children, especially those born to women who had moved to urban areas to conceal their pregnancy, were neither registered nor baptised, the attempt to conceal prompted by fear of exposure and of the Poor Law system.

Also, in urban areas anonymity was known to be easier to achieve because the registration of births, marriages and deaths was harder to enforce in poor and overcrowded districts, and in the early days after 1837, there was less compulsion built into the system anyway. This would account for the frustration some family historians feel when they trace a person back only so far, but are completely unable to trace the person further through their early life.

Some of these unrecorded children will have died young, perhaps as a result of their precarious beginnings, or been abandoned to become foundlings. Rather than being displaced children, this group are probably better described as lost. Christoph Bernoulli, another nineteenth century population theorist, wrote, 'It is beyond doubt that fewer illegitimate children grow up to maturity; that they get through the world with more trouble; that more of them are poor; and that therefore more of them become criminals.' The pressures on these lost and displaced children were almost insurmountable.

The 'Fallen Woman'
By the middle of the nineteenth century, disapproval of the unmarried mother and of her children was at a height, but rather than take practical steps to elevate the women and their offspring from the gutters of society, most of the single mothers were left to make their own arrangements. The term 'fallen woman' was commonly used for women with illegitimate children, or indeed any woman who was known to have had a sexual relationship outside marriage. But disapproving commentators and social activists split fallen women into two groups: those who were 'once fallen' and those who had fallen more than once, in other words likely to have had more than one illegitimate child. For a long time, those who went to

any agency or charity for help were more likely to receive assistance if they were once fallen and there was a greater chance of redemption, but all of them faced an unappetising list of choices.

Many of these options were repellent, not only to modern sensibilities but to those of most contemporary citizens, although it is a testament to the desperation of not just the families of the mother, but of the woman herself that they or she felt compelled to try them. All the usual condemnations of the Church and society would weigh down upon all those involved; a woman who found herself in the position of single parent in the mid-nineteenth century was a far cry from the relatively well supported single parents of the late twentieth century, for whom the stigma of having an illegitimate child is so much less.

'A Fate Worse Than Death': Solutions to the Unwanted Pregnancy
The safest solution to the plight of any woman who found herself single and pregnant was to marry the father, or just find a husband who would take her and the child on. Bearing in mind that a significant percentage – possibly over a third – of all brides in the mid-nineteenth century were pregnant on their wedding day, clearly this was an option that worked for many, and it is a curiosity of many family histories that women who 'had to get married' were later on brutal in their condemnation of daughters who found themselves in the same predicament.

The respectability that marriage instantly brought, whether it was a happy union or not, was regarded as a cure-all and these girls were seen as having manufactured a success out of a disaster. However, women who failed to secure their husband, who had had a union with a married man, or had been the victim of rape or abuse, were regarded as failures both morally and pragmatically. The fact that the marriage was a 'just in time' ceremony seemed to be irrelevant; it was securing the father, or indeed any man, that mattered. There are many thousands of examples of 'just in time' marriages recorded in family histories, and this is one very typical case.

Sometime around the beginning of 1863, in Birmingham, a young woman named Mary Ann Freeman became pregnant. She lived in Essex Street, one of the poorest streets in the centre of the city, with her mother, two female lodgers and a nine-year-old boy described as the mother's grandson. No men, as breadwinners, had lived in this household for at least 12 years, although a variety of daughters, grandchildren and female lodgers came and went. Mary Ann was not married, but on this occasion she was lucky. She married Andrew Wilson on 28 June 1863, well into the third trimester of her pregnancy, and presumably was visibly pregnant when she walked into St Luke's Church for the marriage ceremony.

On 2 September, little Edward Henry was born and was duly registered as the child of a married couple. There is nothing in this story to suggest that Edward was not the son of Andrew Wilson, so as historians we have to take the documentary evidence at face value and accept that Andrew was indeed the baby's father. Mary was fortunate; she came from a desperately poor household which survived on the meagre pickings that outworking (in this case, linen button covering) could provide women on their own, so there was no guarantee that her all-female family could have supported her and the baby. She would have been a prime candidate for the workhouse, or prostitution. As it was, she lived for many decades with her husband Andrew who seemed always to have work, went on to have more children, and presumably they were as comfortable as any labouring family could be in the second half of the nineteenth century.

The adult Edward went on to marry and unlike his parents, waited till after his wedding to start his own family of nine children – a stereotypically large Victorian family. As to whether Mary Ann and Andrew were 'happy' in a romantic sense, one will never know, and it was probably never part of the package anyway – security and survival were more likely to be priorities than emotion, as well as making sure that Mary's first born was not one of the 6 per cent of registered babies born outside marriage. The Royal Commission, which had examined the state of the bastardy laws prior to the 1834 Poor Law Amendment Act, put such marriages of convenience in starker terms. They commented that such marriages were 'founded not on affection, not on esteem, not on the prospect of providing for a family, but on fear on one side and vice on both'. One hopes that for Mary and her husband, the marital relationship was not quite that bleak.

Widows left trying to cope without their man were equally pragmatic. Caroline Bardsley had a daughter at the age of 19 in January 1872, and was not married. However, she was living with one Dan Bowker and when she went to register the birth of Mary Ellen, she told the registrar she was married to Dan – so that the birth certificate of her daughter would look 'respectable', and her daughter would not have to be stigmatised all her life by an honest admission that her mother had not been married at the time of the birth. Almost exactly nine months later, Caroline and Dan travelled from Haughton Green, then on the outskirts of East Manchester, to the register office in central Manchester and went through a civil marriage ceremony. They could not marry in their own locality, as Caroline had already let it be known that she *was* married, and all this subterfuge was to save face for her daughter and for herself.

It was to little avail, however, as the following year, Dan died of tuberculosis and she was left the penniless widow of a labourer in a hat factory. What would a woman in her position do now? She was only 21 years old, fit and well, but how could she work and keep her daughter? There was rent to pay and food to buy. The prospect of going into the workhouse, leaving her daughter with a thoughtless childminder who would dope her baby with opiates, or having to give up her daughter, must have loomed large for Caroline. She was far enough away from her own family not to be able to rely on support from them, and in any case she had no sisters who might be able to help by taking on the baby at least for the time being.

For many women – and men – left widowed with young children to look after, a pragmatic solution was the obvious one: find another spouse, and that is what she did. Just eight weeks after Dan Bowker died, Caroline took herself off to Stockport, again out of her immediate locality – and married John Stopford, a farmer who was her neighbour and eleven years her senior. While it may sound rather unseemly to marry again so soon (and Caroline may have felt this too, which is why she went to Stockport for the wedding even though there were places of worship closer than that she could have used), it was very much a matter of practicalities. Caroline and her child needed support, and that support was best found in the long-term solution of a new husband – now, Caroline's baby was no longer an orphan and her future was relatively secure once again.

Caroline herself was one of nine children, the same number of children as Queen Victoria had, but it is highly unlikely that labouring families would have regarded themselves as in any way akin to the monarch and her brood (pictured in Plate 3). Queen Victoria's many images of her happy and large family were widely promoted as the ideal family of the day, despite the fact that middle-class couples were starting to practise contraception by the late nineteenth century. When Victoria's consort, Prince Albert, died, although the Queen was bereft and heartbroken, her life continued on as before in a material sense. For the likes of Caroline, to lose the main breadwinner, usually one's male partner, was a catastrophe.

Other women tried to terminate their pregnancy by using a variety of ad hoc methods, many of which persisted well into the 1960s. These were almost always of dubious efficacy, the successful reputation of some most likely achieved by a coincidental miscarriage. Jumping off furniture, moving heavy furniture, running up and down stairs, sitting in a bath of very hot water and drinking large amounts of gin, using Slippery Elm bark, or caustic soda solutions, or metal objects soaked in vinegar to create an abortive solution, and various sharp implements were of course highly dangerous and could result in death.

As late as the mid-twentieth century (but generally before the Abortion Act of 1967), nurses on duty in gynaecological wards referred to Friday evenings as 'Slippery Elm Night', as they struggled to deal with the influx of emergency cases caused by these home 'remedies'. Friday night was a popular choice to try to end a pregnancy as it gave the woman the weekend to recover before work again on Monday. Going to the local abortionist did not reduce the risks of shock, infection or haemorrhage; in fact, it probably compounded them.

The later the term of the pregnancy, the higher the risks. In the nineteenth century, a woman was reliant on knowing her own body and cycle well enough to detect the pregnancy early enough to do something about it. Other women would wait until the 'quickening', in other words, when they were sure they had felt the baby moving around in the womb, to decide if they were pregnant – astonishingly poor levels of understanding of their own bodies would not have helped matters.

In 1846, a 40-year-old woman named Mary Ledger who lived with her daughter and two grandchildren in Nottingham, died as a result of trying to procure a late abortion. Mary was separated from her husband but had previously been in a relationship with another man. It is not known what she did, or took, but on becoming ill, she sent for a midwife and delivered a baby of 16 weeks' gestation. This was on a Monday – Mary's condition continued to deteriorate until she passed away the following Saturday, and it was accepted at the inquest that the miscarriage was self induced and was the cause of her death.

The *Nottingham Guardian*, which had reported Mary's death, also named an abortionist from another case from earlier that year. Her name was Mary Goodall and she was sentenced to two years' imprisonment for working as an abortionist. There was no proof that she had received money for her services, but had there been, she would have been transported to Australia.

There is a popular belief that Victorian morality would not allow for the promotion of any product which aided miscarriage, but early women's magazines, such as the *Englishwoman's Domestic Magazine* begun in 1852 by Mrs Isabella Beeton (author of the *Book of Household Management*, published in 1861) and her publisher husband, contained obliquely worded advertisements for discreetly wrapped products that could cure all 'women's ailments' – which any female reader of the magazine knew, would include unwanted pregnancies. One of the main ingredients was usually a quantity of Pennyroyal, a medicinal herb, which even today carries a warning for pregnant women regarding its handling because of its capacity to induce miscarriage.

Such adverts, which included hints that the product was 'restorative' (in other words would restore one's menstrual cycle to regularity) were undoubtedly not the type of genteel scientific education the Beetons were trying to promote to lower-middle-class Englishwomen at the time, but women of any social class could fall prey to an unwanted pregnancy, either in or outside of marriage. After 1861 abortion – whether induced by drugs or surgery – was illegal following the Offences Against the Person Act. Under this act, if the woman died as a result of the 'treatment', it was henceforward treated as manslaughter, which was a capital offence.

Unfortunately, this just pushed the abortionists further under cover and it is unlikely that it deterred many of them from carrying out their trade, such was the demand in an era when few adults understood, or had access to, methods of contraception. Over a century had yet to elapse before any woman in England and Wales could obtain a legal abortion in discreet circumstances, yet safe and clinical conditions.

Many women too frightened to try the above remedies, or who had left it too late, may have thrown themselves on the mercy of their family. Many working-class families closed ranks and the illegitimate baby was quietly absorbed into the family circles. He or she may be 'given' to a childless relative, a grandparent, or raised as yet another child of the mother of the single mother – so that the child's mother was, to the outside world, her or his sibling. If the family had refused to have her in the house while she was pregnant, the mother could apply to go into the workhouse and have her baby there, and in some cases the family may well have taken her back in after the birth.

It was also possible for a working single mother to find a baby minder to take the child while she went to work in a factory or workshop, sometimes known as 'putting out' the child, as was famously quoted in Friedrich Engels' book, *The Condition of the Working Class in England in 1844*: 'Dr Hawkins, Commissioner (Factories Inquiry) for Lancashire, expresses his opinion as follows: "The mother is more than twelve hours away from her child daily; the baby is cared for by a young girl or an old woman, to whom it is given to nurse."'

Consequently, some of the Lancashire mill workers were able to hang on to their babies and still work, and childminders did not seem to discriminate between the legitimate and illegitimate children they provided day 'care' for. As a result, many single women could be mothers and keep their jobs in the factories and mills, but it was still a less than satisfactory solution bearing in mind the high percentages of childminded babies who died in infancy.

Most of these mothers accepted that baby minders would dose the babies with laudanum or the infamous Godfrey's Cordial (originally a teething soother which usually contained large quantities of an opiate) so that they would stay docile during the day, but this had the disadvantage of making the baby too groggy to feed when their mother came for them and could lead to a failure to thrive, addiction to the opiates, and eventually death (a very similar chain of events to those which resulted from the deliberate mistreatment of babies by baby farmers). If the baby survived the ministrations of the childminder, compulsory education, as finally enforced by the 1880 Education Act, could take over and go a long way to solving the mother's childcare problems. In many industrial areas children sometimes started school at a younger age than in rural areas, because of the pressure working mothers were under.

But what if the mother of the illegitimate baby had no family support, or the support of her family was conditional on the baby not being around any more? The other stumbling block was work; a working-class or poor woman needed to feed herself, and for many women a baby was a passport to the workhouse because she would lose her position if she tried to work and keep, or even conceal, a baby. Not all women worked in industrial settings, in factories and mills – for many women, especially domestic servants and farm labourers, it was a different story, as their jobs often required them to live in and also pull their weight in very physically arduous work, so a pregnancy was almost certain to mean loss of position. If a woman had not been able to induce a miscarriage and she now had a baby that could eventually lead to her starvation and ruin, she could well be tempted to dispose of the child completely.

Selling the child oneself was one option. In 1870, a woman walked into a public house in Market Street, Sheffield, carrying in her arms a beautiful and bonny baby. A local farmer commented on the baby and said he wished he had a fine baby like that for his own, upon which the woman offered to sell the baby to him. After some more conversation, the baby was sold to the farmer for half a sovereign, about 10s. or the equivalent of £216 today. The farmer, delighted with his purchase, called a cab and went home with the baby. The next day, the mother regretted her decision to sell her baby and went looking for the farmer. She searched high and low for the man and her child, even involving the police, but a week later she was no further in her search.

The reasons why this woman sold her baby are not known, but she did so without knowing anything about the farmer, his character or his circumstances. It was either an act of complete desperation, or complete callousness, but she was not alone in choosing this course of action. Many women must have felt that to sell the child to someone who seemed willing to show it affection, or even just give it a home, was preferable to paying someone to 'adopt' the child, on the basis that if someone would part with money for the child, they must think she or he was worth investing in. However, if the mother was so desperate that she did not give any thought at all as to the character of the purchaser, she would not think through the implications of an affluent person wanting to take a child from a poor background, and unwittingly sell the child into a life of drudgery or even slavery and abuse.

Another solution was to abandon the baby or young child, either by exposing it, leaving it anonymously outside a workhouse, hospital or orphanage, or simply placing it in a street at a quiet time. The image in Plate 1 from *The Pictorial Times* of 1846, epitomises the doom-laden public perception of the desperate single mother. Here, the swaddled baby is left alone under a tree, in a remote place, while the mother – the 'Fallen Woman', that great preoccupation of moral campaigners of the period – has collapsed to her knees in the background, with her arms raised to the heavens. This was certainly one way of relinquishing all responsibility for the illegitimate child.

Some women simply could not cope with the stigma of being an unmarried mother and sank so low in spirits that they took their own life. In Billington, Lancashire in September 1854, a young woman named Maria Clegg took her own life and that of her illegitimate baby. The local newspaper, the *Chronicle*, reported the tragedy as follows:

> *An inquest on view of the bodies ... was held at the Petre's Arms in Billington ... the deceased woman was unmarried, and the birth of the illegitimate child seems to have preyed upon her spirits. She was left in the house on Wednesday evening with the child. Her brother returned about seven o'clock, after milking, and missed the deceased. A search was made, and the bodies were found in a large water butt at the back of the house. Life was quite extinct. The infant was locked in the arms of its mother. There is no doubt that it was her own act. She had been low in spirits for some time. A verdict of 'Temporary Insanity' was returned.*

It is unlikely that anyone bothered to ask poor Maria how she was feeling, and of course the treatment of mental health issues such as postnatal depression were then little understood. Indeed, at this time, psychiatry was an unheard-of profession whose development was still in the future. However, whatever the cause of the mental anguish which led her to take her own and her baby's life, it is highly probable that the isolation and stigma of being a lone mother at this time would have been a contributing factor in her decision.

For single mothers who had the confidence to do so (or who had family willing to help them), a private claim for maintenance could be made. This might take the form of a private arrangement, drawn up by a local solicitor. One such arrangement took place in June 1907 in North Wales, between John Francis Robinson and Mabel Flora Owens. It was drawn up and overseen by a firm of solicitors in Conwy town and followed a standard format: after stating that the unnamed illegitimate baby that had recently been born was the child of the two parties concerned, in particular stating that John Robinson was the father, it goes on to say that the father was to pay 3s 6d (approximately £18 today) per week for the child's maintenance until she or he reached the age of fourteen; he was also instructed to pay five guineas (£5 5s – the equivalent of about £550 today) towards the costs of the birth and the legal costs of drawing up the agreement.

Miss Owens was to retain custody of the child and she agreed to provide the child with 'sufficient food, clothing, lodging and medical attendance'; she must also refrain from any further claims or legal proceedings against the father beyond the current agreement, and 'shall not in any way molest or disturb the said J.F. Robinson nor in any way communicate to other persons nor make it public the fact that the said child is a child of the said J.F. Robinson'.

This type of private agreement has two advantages: firstly it secures the future of the illegitimate child and allows her or him to stay with the mother, with a very modest income; secondly, it keeps the identity of the father a secret, and ensures that the matter will not be taken through any more public legal proceedings. There must have been many hundreds of these private arrangements made, not all, of course, through a solicitor as this one was; some would not even have had any paperwork to reinforce them. At least, if they were adhered to, the illegitimate children concerned may well have been saved from either being passed around the family as a helpless little nomad, and it certainly kept them from ending up in the workhouse or orphanage.

The option of applying for an affiliation order against the father still remained, although the 1868 Poor Law Amendment Act took a retrograde step and restored the powers of the Poor Law Guardians to institute proceedings against a putative father with a view to obtaining maintenance for the illegitimate child. However, the law still required the mother to give corroborating evidence of paternity in person, which left the burden of proof still with her.

Straightforward infanticide, other than exposure of the baby, was often disguised as an accident; mothers would claim that they had the baby in bed with them, cuddled up, and awoke in the morning to find they had lain on the baby in the night and it had suffocated – an event known as 'overlaying'. In 1861 alone, over 1,100 inquests were held just in London for young children who had died from unexplained or violent causes, and it was claimed that this figure was increasing year by year. The rise was attributed to two factors – the inability of the mother to maintain her child, and the shame of having illegitimate offspring. Sometimes the finger of blame was pointed at the law, because at this time a single mother could only obtain 2s 6d per week from the father of the child, which was not nearly enough to maintain the child and was not a contribution to the costs of the lying-in or antenatal care. Much debate over 'hidden' homicides raged in the mid-nineteenth century, with acrimonious exchanges and discussion between the nation's doctors and the coroners' service.

Another method was to hand over the baby to an adoptive or foster parent, or nurse, who would hopefully treat the child as lovingly as their own for as long as necessary, even for life. Such arrangements were without legal basis at this time, and are rarely documented, but were often hoped for. Sometimes a desperate family or individual would advertise for new parents for the child, as in this case from the *Western Gazette* of 15 February 1901:

> *Adoption. Would anyone, in really good circumstances, ADOPT, without any reward whatever, a well-born ORPHAN BABY BOY? A most sad case. – Write Box 170, Gazette Office, Yeovil.*

It would be impossible now to ascertain whether this baby was truly an orphan or a straightforward case of an illegitimate child whose mother wanted it to be discreetly passed on to a new family, but what is really significant is the desire to have the baby adopted 'without any reward whatever'. This is a clear attempt to distinguish these circumstances from advertisements which usually conformed to the wording of the three examples below:

> *Child wanted, to Adopt, with premium. –*
> *G.H., Box 63, Telegraph Office, Sheffield.*
> (From the *Sheffield Daily Telegraph*, 9 June 1903)

> *CARE of CHILD or would ADOPT;*
> *lady could have apartments during accouchement. –*
> *A., care of 30 Pretoria-avenue, High-street, Walthamstow.*
> (From the *Chelmsford Chronicle*, 5 April 1889)

> *Wanted a child to adopt; small premium required;*
> *address Mrs Bolton, Post-office, Leeds.*
> (From *Edinburgh Evening News*, 24 February 1880)

Baby Farming

Advertisements such as the three above were about as far from a happy adoption solution as it is possible to get, but to a desperate single or expectant mother they were a lifeline, as they were all placed in provincial newspapers by individuals who became widely known as baby farmers.

To 'farm out' a baby or child meant that the birth parent/s or family were effectively sub-contracting out the role of parent to another, in this case, a person who for a sum of money, either all paid up front or in instalments over weeks or occasionally monthly, would then take care of the child for the mother ostensibly on a indefinite basis or until such time as the mother was in a position to reclaim the child. Sometimes, the understanding was that the baby farmer would act as a broker, and foster the child until she or he could arrange a permanent adoption for it.

Single women without family support, who wanted to maintain contact with their baby but at the same time needed to work, perhaps in positions such as domestic service where it was impossible to keep a child, would make contact with the advertiser and arrange to hand over the child to their safe keeping. Other women went through this procedure with the financial and practical support of relatives. The handover often took place in a public place, such as a railway station, with a sum of money in full payment or as deposit being made at the same time. The baby farmer would give full assurances to the mother that the baby would be looked after like her own and that regular letters would be sent telling of baby's progress. In most cases, there would be little or no further contact between birth mother and child, although the mother would continue to send money for the upkeep of the baby.

What happened after this parting could vary. Sometimes, the baby never made it to the baby farmer's address; it was abandoned on the way home. If it was taken home, it would more than likely be stripped of its own clothes which would be pawned or sold, placed in a rudimentary bed such as an old drawer or wooden fruit box, and placed in a room with several other 'farmed' babies. Her/his routine would consist of being fed occasionally with a poor mix of artificial food such as cow's milk padded out with completely inappropriate substances such as chalk – and almost invariably laced with an opiate-based substance to keep the child quiet.

The most widely used of these potions was the notorious Godfrey's Cordial, a typical receipt for which is as follows:

Liquid Opium	*1 drachm*
Carraway oil	*4 drops*
Spirits of Juniper	*4 drops*
Tincture of Ginger	*2 drachms*
Essence of Aniseed	*2 drachms*
Liquid burnt sugar	*2 drachms*
Liquid Liquorice extract	*4 drachms*
Simple syrup	*4 drachms to 10 ounces*

[One drachm is roughly the equivalent to one-eighth of a fluid ounce.]

An established opiate-based product (it is known to have been on the market as far back as the eighteenth century), Godfrey's Cordial was widely used in very small amounts for the legitimate purpose of calming babies who were teething, or fractious because of illness and so on, but baby farmers used it round the clock to keep babies quiet and to make sure that neighbours had no inkling of the activities going on in the baby farmer's house. It also led to the child becoming addicted to this 'stupefactive' as they were known, lethargic, failing to thrive and unable to feed even if offered real nourishment.

Hygiene was usually non-existent, and there were rarely regular attempts to clean the baby or change its napkin (if it had one at all). Illness and death almost inevitably followed, but naturally this was not reported to the birth mother, who would continue to pay for a child who no longer lived, sometimes on the basis of continued receipt of fictitious enthusiastic letters from the baby farmer telling of baby's growth and development. The rudimentary care given to these abused children would deteriorate still further if the baby farmer herself became as addicted to the potion as the babies were – as was the case with Amelia Dyer, the most notorious and prolific of the known baby farmers.

A variation to the services offered by baby farmers is mentioned in the advertisement placed by the baby farmer in Walthamstow – accommodation and midwifery services ('accouchement') for the expectant mother, especially useful for those whose families had cast them out of the family home or for those who had lost their employment. This meant that one could pay for a room at the baby farmer's establishment and the baby farmer would either attend the birth herself, or provide a 'midwife'. Once the baby was born, she/he would be quickly taken into the baby farming part of the enterprise, and the mother could leave to begin her life anew.

An inquest reported in the *Liverpool Mercury* in September 1879 is fairly typical of the provincial baby farming activities which came to light as a result of prosecutions. One John Barnes and his wife were arrested for having been found with three emaciated and filthy babies aged 5, 9 and 15 months in their home in Church Road, Higher Tranmere on the Wirral. There was no food in the house beyond a loaf of bread and no bed clothes for the children. After the police had entered the house, the medical officer of Birkenhead Workhouse was summoned, and he decreed that the children should be removed to the workhouse for their own safety and to be treated.

At least two of these infants died as a result of the neglect and abuse they had been subjected to, and on investigating further, the police found more than 72 documents in the Tranmere house relating to these babies and to several others who had been in the care of the Barnes, including several insurance policies for the children with the Prudential and Victoria Societies. There were numerous letters regarding the baby farming activities, one being an agreement drawn up by Mrs Barnes for the sum of £30 to be handed over by the birth mother for the care of her baby.

There is no hint of sensationalism in the reporter's tone as he recounted what the coroner had to say about the case:

> [the authorities] ... *did not know how the prisoners were paid or renumerated for the maintenance of the children. If they were renumerated by receiving a weekly allowance sufficient to maintain the children and also to compensate them for their trouble, there would be some motive for keeping the children in a healthy and proper manner. It might, however be pointed out that the prisoners received a lump sum, and in that case there was, as a matter of course, a motive to get rid of the children as quickly as possible.*

Clearly, the Barnes were using both lump sums and instalment payments as part of their baby farming business. This is a relatively unusual case in that husband and wife were seen as equally culpable, and they were sentenced to life imprisonment for their 'cruelties and crimes of the most revolting character', reported the *Lloyds Weekly Newspaper* of 2 November 1879. The majority of convicted baby farmers were female, although there is evidence that other members of the family often were fully aware of what went on and even helped out and benefited from the financial gain – the husband and daughter of Amelia Dyer being two individuals who witnessed and profited from it. Indeed, Dyer's daughter went on to become a baby farmer of sorts herself, hardly surprising that after having her own childhood warped by the child abuse she had witnessed (but did not suffer from herself), she would also become an abuser.

While cases such as the Barnes in Tranmere usually proved inconclusive enough to result in a murder charge – at this time it was not easy to prove exactly how and why a baby had failed to thrive and died – numerous baby farmers met the death penalty and were hanged: Amelia Dyer in 1896; Margaret Waters in 1870; Ada Chard Williams in 1900; and Leslie James in 1907 (the only woman in Wales to suffer the death penalty in the twentieth century) are a few examples.

Others, such as Charlotte Winsor of Torquay, received sentences of life imprisonment, and Elizabeth Dearden of Morecambe received a sentence of six months' imprisonment in May 1901 for baby farming and for, as the newspapers put it, 'subletting' two of the babies to a woman in Kendal. Interestingly, the Magistrates in Lancaster also censured one of Dearden's clients, a mother of twins from Reading, for handing over £65 to have her infant twins farmed out to Dearden – a sign that there was disapproval not only of the baby farmers, but of their clients too, for encouraging this distasteful practice.

Public Outcry

More and more baby farming court cases were appearing in the newspapers and the reaction of the public was typically one of outrage and disgust, and one can imagine appalled middle Englanders reading reports of the maltreated babies, their 'immoral' mothers and the criminals who took the children with a sense that certainly for the adults, the various punishments were no more than they deserved; while the national opinion was more like a collective guilt that one of the world's great nations could allow this to occur in its midst.

Newspapers did their bit in driving the campaign for official action on this matter. The *Hull Packet* and *East Riding Times* reported on a baby farming case in London with a commendably sombre tone – the case was that of a two-week-old baby boy handed to a Mrs Cooper, who bears all the credentials for a baby farmer, by his affluent single mother. She told the baby farmer that she and the father of the baby wished him to be adopted out to a permanent and loving family as they were to be married and emigrate to Australia, and she handed over a bundle of extremely good quality clothes (including an outdoor outfit of 'a scarlet dress and Scotch cap, with a white feather') and £10 for the 'adoption fee'. Of course, the baby failed to thrive and died.

There is nothing exceptional about this story as far as baby farming goes, but the comment from the reporter is interesting:

> *The system of getting rid of the embarrassment of unwanted children by 'adoption' appears to be well organised and to be in process of development into an extensive branch of trade. It is said by medical men who have opportunities of becoming acquainted with such matters that children are 'adopted' out by scores. When the premium is paid to the adopting parents the child is registered in their name (at least, this is the general practice), and then, if the child dies either from disease ... or from accident, such as overlaying &c, resulting in suffocation ... disagreeable ... suspicions are obviated. There is, of course, as everybody knows, a fine of £50 provided for the offence of making false representations to the registrar. But as all the parties to the transaction are deeply interested in keeping it a close secret, it need hardly be said that the penalty is never enforced in such cases.*

The article goes on to call for the registration of all those who take in children to nurse (in a sense, fostering) or adopt, and also calls for the closer regulation of the registration of infants.

Also in the 1860s, Dr Ernest Hart undertook an impassioned campaign against baby farming with a series of articles in the *British Medical Journal* (BMJ) and even after the Infant Life Protection Act of 1872, he was still making his point, here in the BMJ of 14 December 1878:

One would have thought that, since the exposure of the practice of baby farmers a few years ago, the knowledge then gained would have been sufficient to have influenced a coroner to hold an inquest in a case such as this ... a medical practitioner was asked to visit a house ... to see if a child were dead. He ... found the child dead ... it was quite well previously, and had not had any medical attendance. It was a nurse child aged twelve months ... the woman having charge of it a cripple, and had one or two other such children under her care. There was ... enough primae facie evidence that the woman wished to get rid of her profitless encumbrance.

In this case, Dr Hart reports further that the doctor concerned contacted the coroner as he felt the case worthy of investigation, but the coroner replied that there was 'no reason to suppose that the death of the child arose from anything but natural causes' and later added that he thought the child had had 'bronchitis and it had gone to its head' – hardly the basis for a scientific conclusion. Dr Hart's fury was directed partly at the coroners who refused, in his view, to take the deaths of such children seriously, thereby encouraging the boldness of the baby farmers in finishing off their charges, and also at local authorities who failed to use the 1872 Act to apply the new registration of baby minders and paid foster parents, to exclude those who could not or would not carry out suitable childcare in appropriate surroundings or who did not have good characters.

One final case explicitly ties the practice of baby farming in with the concept of adoption, and indeed with numerous other issues around childbirth, illegitimacy and cruelty to children and infants. In London at the beginning of 1893, an inquiry into the death of nine-week-old Albert Victor Weston was held. Albert was passed to one Ellen Barnard as a 'nurse-child' but was in fact destined to become a 'farmed' baby. For a payment of £2, Albert was handed over at Victoria Station in London by a Mrs Weston and taken back to the Barnard household where, like other farmed babies there, he was fed on milk, oatmeal and barley water. He failed to thrive and died, and a post-morten revealed that he was grossly underweight and had effectively died of starvation.

Mrs Weston's real name was Sarah Baker, wife of a railway porter. She had numerous other aliases, as did the ladies who went to stay with her for the accouchement or lying-in – Baker stated that the ladies also gave what name they liked. Once the babies were born, advertisements were placed in newspapers for them to be adopted – these adverts were paid for by the mothers. Presumably, those who were not adopted stayed at the baby farm in another part of the house.

The most severe verdict was given against Ellen Barnard, who was convicted of manslaughter, although the jury considered that Baker was more morally at fault and requested that the coroner should severely censure her.

This is a fascinating example of a case involving two baby farmers, and it would seem that the public had a clear perception of what adverts such as these implied (the eventual death of the child) and laid the blame at the feet of the people who chose to exploit this service. Neither woman had any thought for the welfare of the baby.

As the appearance of legislation protecting children, such as the Infant Life Protection Acts of 1872 and 1897, and the Children Act of 1908, made inroads into the reduction of the baby farming industry, and legitimate charity-based accommodation for unwanted children became more readily available, this unpleasant practice faded into the background. The 1872 Act was, first and foremost, concerned to protect the lives of children fostered out or placed in baby farms.

As a result of the Act, baby farmers had to be registered, and licensed with the local authority, deaths of infants had to be reported within 24 hours and a doctor's certificate obtained, otherwise an inquest would follow automatically – this would also be a useful safeguard against infanticide and overlaying. The law applied to all those receiving for reward, two or more children under the age of one year, for more than 24 hours. The person had to be of good character, have a decent home, and be able to maintain the child or children. Unfortunately, the act did not cover farmed-out single children, for which it was criticised.

However, baby farming did have opportunities to make a comeback in a minor way as a result of the *carpe diem* attitude of the two World Wars, which led to an upsurge in the birth of unwanted babies. One such baby was the result of an affair that a young woman had while working as a typist in a munitions works during the First World War. Named Kathleen, the baby was placed with Walter and Lydia Elius in Carmarthenshire, where, true to form, she eventually disappeared from sight. Various excuses were given including that her mother had claimed her, that she had died and been thrown into the river, and that she had died and been buried in sand.

It is unlikely that the truth about little Kathleen will ever be known, although the couple were eventually sentenced to five years' imprisonment each for the manslaughter of another baby who was found wrapped up and weighted in the River Gwendraeth. Clearly, although baby farming had been undermined by improvements or changes in the care of unwanted children over the previous 50 years, when there was dire need, it could still make a profitable income for the unscrupulous, and much more needed to be done to co-ordinate and make available a better system of child protection. One such method, claimed campaigners at the time, was to legalise adoption.

Baby farming was a world shrouded in secrecy – it is extremely difficult to find any records of the baby farming 'industry' other than those in the newspapers, court cases and other official records. After all, what birth mother would offer her own story for the public to read, and risk the condemnation of the Victorian moral majority – especially if, as with some of the clients of Amelia Dyer, she had put her antipathy towards her baby in writing in a letter to the baby farmer, and had deliberately put the baby into this care with reasonable knowledge that it would not survive? There can be little doubt that many baby farmers did not need to advertise, but found plenty of ready clients simply by word of mouth, such was the need to find a way to dispose of an unwanted baby.

Historians must be careful not to be all-encompassing in their condemnation of the practice of baby farming. Even though by the end of the nineteenth century, baby farming had firmly linked the word 'adoption' with the criminal treatment of children, the London authorities tried to appropriate it to good use by farming out babies and small children to families in outer London in an attempt to get the children out of the workhouse environment, so that they could experience family life as far as was possible. There must have been some childminders and informal foster parents who loved their charges dearly and looked after them well, but they are not the ones who found themselves in the news.

In addition, it would be wrong to assume that all the babies passed to baby farmers were from poor families; indeed if the family could raise and hand over lump sums of at least £10 or more (there are examples of up to £50 changing hands for one baby), they were more likely to be aspirant working class or middle class. While there can be no excuse for the appalling and upsetting levels of child abuse which occurred in baby farming, the bleak financial outlook for poor working-class women, most of whom only had their domestic and mothering skills to sell, must have encouraged them to use these skills to take advantage of other women's vulnerability as the only way they could earn large amounts of cash relatively easily outside of prostitution.

Of course, some of the baby farmers were habitual law breakers – Leslie James, the Cardiff baby farmer (real name Rhoda Willis) had been a convicted petty thief, sex worker, an alcoholic and neglectful of her own children to the point where they were taken from her by her in-laws. Amelia Dyer showed all the signs of being addicted to opiate-based medicines and alcohol. Profoundly distasteful though these women were, as a group they suffered harsher penalties than some other criminal groups, such as biological mothers who killed their children, and this may have been because they had diverted so strongly from the contemporary ideal of the angel in the house, the devoted mother and assiduous homemaker. They were, in that sense, beyond the control of the society they inhabited.

One of the key positive outcomes of the public outcry regarding baby farming, was that it became crystal clear that some form of governing body or organisation was needed to control or at least oversee the process of handing over a child from one family to another; in that sense it was a deeply saddening, but necessary prompt in the direction of formalised adoption.

For children and babies who were passed on to the new 'adoptive' parents with a large sum of money, but who did not remain with one person, becoming part of a 'trade' in babies was one unpleasant outcome. A baby acquired with a lump sum of £50, might be sold on for £25 with the other half being kept; adoptive 'parent' number two might then sell the baby for £12 and keep the rest, and so on down the line until the baby had no financial worth left. Its fate at that point, as a worthless commodity, was bleak.

Clearly then, the trade in babies touched all strata of society, as the following case of fraud illustrates. In 1878, the extraordinary case of Lady Gooch caused much comment in the press and reads like a classic Victorian melodrama. Annie Louise was the wife of Sir Francis Gooch and desperately wanted a child of her own, if only to secure her husband's fortune, which, if the couple remained childless, would revert to another relative of her husband's.

47

Apparently unable to conceive herself, Lady Gooch proceeded to tell her husband's tenants and anyone else who would listen, that she was indeed with child and then approached the family surgeon and asked him to help her find a baby to pass off as her own. She told Mr Worthington, the surgeon, that she had believed herself to be pregnant but then found she was not and was afraid to tell her husband. It would seem she was padding her body to make herself look pregnant, and suggested to the doctor that he attend her at her home and pretend to deliver a baby. In the meantime Lady Gooch would make arrangements in London to obtain a baby boy to become her unwitting husband's son and heir.

The surgeon naturally refused and tried to talk her out of the scheme, and asked why she could not openly adopt a child? The answer was that only the natural child of the couple would secure the property and titles, which shows how important an affluent family's pedigree was to them. Mr Worthington sent his 'patient' away with the threat that if she tried to embroil him any further, he would tell her husband of her plans.

Meanwhile, during the 'pregnancy' Lady Gooch visited the 'Refuge for Deserted Mothers and Their Infants' in Great Coram Street, London, ironically a street named after the founder of the famous and highly reputable Foundling Hospital, Thomas Coram. It was administered by a matron, Mrs Palmer, and was an establishment known to have babies available for adoption. Lady Gooch was to have a baby brought from Peckham to the home specifically to be adopted, but no record of the handover was made in the home's books. The matron later stated under oath she did not know Lady Gooch's name or marital status, adding that it was not her business to know, but on 28 October, Lady Gooch walked out of the Home with a two-week-old baby boy as her own child. Eventually, her plot was uncovered and her story became national news.

What was extraordinary about the story of Lady Gooch and the refuge was that she was able to obtain a baby so easily and anonymously, and for what were seen as fraudulent purposes. The idea of a home where babies were kept and then passed on to new families as adopted children was no surprise at all to the public. Indeed, this particular home was highly respectable, being run by a council of ladies of rank including the Dowager Lady Monteagle, the Hon. Mrs V. Johnson, and Mrs Bonham Carter. It was primarily a refuge for generally reputable young women who had 'fallen' for the first time and had an illegitimate baby. The girls went away for their confinement and returned to the home with their baby, some of whom would be adopted out and others kept at the home. In fact, in 1877 the home arranged for 28 of the babies to be adopted.

Following the trial, a debate arose in the letters page of journals and newspapers as to the character of the home, some calling it no more than a 'baby shop', others likening it to a baby farm, and yet another correspondent describing it as 'an Exchange and Mart for babies'. A Mr Chalmers sprang to the defence of the institution in a letter quoted in the *Englishwoman's Review* of 14 December, describing how it had been set up by Mrs Main who was a former superintendent of a Bible Mission and that only fallen women 'of a generally respectable character' were helped – they were 'in great privation and distress, out of situation, without employment ... unable to earn a living or support their offspring, and in consequence, under strong temptation to infanticide or to a life of profligacy'.

The idea of the home was to provide a safe haven for the babies so that the mothers could return to 'honest industry, support themselves and their children, and in some measure at least, to regain the position and character they had lost.' He went on to say that it was the 'kindest, wisest and most useful' institution of its kind in London and that part of its income came from the hard-earned wages of the mothers (and by comparison, the fathers only contributed about 10 per cent of the amount that the mothers did).

One note of negativity is raised by the supporter, however, which to the modern reader may strike an uneasy chord. Mr Chalmers also claimed that the home had never had to worry about what to do with the babies once they outgrew the home, as 'For first, infants born in such unhappy circumstances are difficult to rear. The anxiety and privations undergone by the mothers prior to the birth too often entail on their offspring a sickly existence; and notwithstanding the tenderest care, and the best medical advice, many are removed by death.' This is a strange point of view for any charitable supporter to take – to accept the infant mortality rate without any comment as to what could be done about it. He goes on to say that of the children who survived, many were returned to their mothers once she had regained some stability in her life. Of the others, many seemed to have been adopted – 'in the last few years upwards of 200 children have been disposed of in this way'.

After expressing surprise that illegitimate children could be popular with adoptive parents, Mr Chalmers put forward the theory that these babies were popular specifically because they had no father in their lives, which meant that the adoptive parents could really believe the child was their very own without fear of a father appearing years hence to claim it. He goes on to extol the benefits of adoption, stating: 'It would be difficult to estimate the good which has thus been secured for these little unfortunates that has been introduced into homes by the filling up of what had been felt to be a painful blank.' Mrs Main, we are told, took great pains to match baby with adoptive parents and that the handing over of the baby was done with 'ceremony and deliberation.' As regards the business of Lady Gooch, Chalmers admits that Mrs Main had been duped, but makes it clear that she would be putting safeguards in place to prevent such a thing happening again.

This story has many of the features of the story of adoption as a whole. Secrecy, illegitimacy, the desire for an heir, a strange indifference to infant mortality, a genuine worthiness on the part of those trying to help, and a determination to obtain redemption for these 'first-fallen' women, are mirrored in many other institutions and campaigns, but most interesting is the absolute acceptance of adoption as a method of creating a new family, and solving a social 'problem' at the same time. Elements of the Victorian passion for 'self help' are here too, with the mothers being encouraged to keep their babies, contribute towards their upkeep, and hopefully take on the babies full-time at some point – echoes also of the later determination of the National Council for the Unmarried Mother and her Child (NCUMC) to support the mother and child, with adoption only as a last resort.

However, not all would-be parents had the money to obtain a baby by offering a large payment. In 1875, a young woman who went by the name of Annie Race was renting rooms in Sandbach, Cheshire, from Mr Roberts, a local grocer. Mr Roberts had several children, including 15-month-old twins. Under pretence of taking one of the children to have a studio photograph taken, Annie went off with the child – and did not come back. She headed for Astbury, then Congleton, and Macclesfield, where she stopped for a rest; she then made her way to Adlington (Cheshire) railway station and bought a ticket for Liverpool, at which point the trail seems to have gone cold. Annie may have stolen the child to order, or so she could sell her or him on, or may just have wanted the child for herself – whatever the reason, child theft (or abduction as it would more likely be called today) was not as rare as it was later to become.

"OUR INNOCENCE IS ALL A SHAM"

It is tempting to think that this next story is about a woman who desperately wanted a child to love as her own and that had her subterfuge not been found out, the baby would have had a happy life. In 1883, a woman going by the name of May Morley or sometimes Cross (neither being her real surname), persuaded a young woman named Eliza Geary to sell her seven-month-old illegitimate baby, George. Morley told Eliza she was acting on behalf of a well-off lady who had one child but could have no more, and who wanted a son to lavish her estate upon. On behalf of the rich lady (who was never identified or seen), Morley promised Eliza £25 (approximately £9,500 today) with which to pay her rent or buy herself a little business, and regular contact to let her know how George was faring.

Despite the baby's grandmother trying to prevent the sale, Eliza went ahead and handed over her baby to Morley at Kings Cross station, walking away in tears with £5 in her pocket and the promise of letters, visits to see George and more money later on. She had also had to sign a declaration which said, 'I, May Morley, receive this child from Eliza Geary to deliver up faithfully to the said lady, and that she shall in future hear from me.' Of course, she never did receive more news of her baby, or any more money, and when her letter asking for news was returned marked 'no known address', she went to the authorities and asked for help.

Eventually, Morley was tracked down to Maidenhead in Berkshire, and Detective Sergeant Summers travelled down there to investigate. He found the baby safe, well and thriving – Morley pointed to him and said, 'There's the baby. You can see we have taken great care of it. The agreement was for the mother to see it every two months, which time is not up yet. I have seen my solicitor in the matter, and the mother should have received a letter from him this morning.' Possibly, the child was going to be sold on to a better-off person, or Morley was genuine in her affection for the child – sadly the outcome is not known, but however it is viewed, it is a highly unsatisfactory way to create an artificial family for oneself.

Some children were fortunate enough in a material sense to be adopted by women who had money and status, but who just happened also to be unmarried. A number of female intellectuals did this, including, in 1888, Constance Maynard, although her adoption experience proved to be complex. For a woman of impeccable middle-class status, successful, affluent and with much to lose, to take on a child of unknown background – essentially a filius populi – was a big statement to make to her status-conscious peers. Constance was the head of Westfield College in London and she chose to adopt a six-year-old girl, Effie.

At the time Constance was 39 years old and of strong Christian faith, and the adoption was purely altruistic and what was more, it crossed class boundaries. In some ways, therefore, it was a bold move by Constance, but sadly it was not a success. On the surface, it appeared that Constance felt she had failed to have an impact on Effie by strengthening her moral and spiritual fibre, and castigated herself for her sometimes ambivalent feelings towards Effie, but apart from blaming herself, she also blamed Effie's parentage (she was part Italian), her egotism, and various other characteristics for the 'failure' of the adoption.

Constance's religious zeal, her depression, and a tendency to treat Effie as her social inferior (for example, by sending her away one summer holiday to work as a servant and giving her second-hand clothes as presents), cannot have helped. For her part, Effie felt undervalued, confused, and as if she did not belong anywhere at all, and was seemingly given little choice as to what she might do with her life. Constance's own social adoptive experiment ended when Effie died of tuberculosis in a workhouse infirmary in 1915. Effie's death as a pauper patient is a sad testament to the low point Constance's feelings for her daughter had sunk to, although Constance was not alone during the period in her failure to appreciate the special emotional needs an adoptive child may have had.

Adoption and Popular Culture

Adoption as a solution to what was seen as a perplexing social problem was well-known enough to feature regularly in different forms of popular culture. Numerous nineteenth-century authors wrote about adoption, and some even adopted a child themselves – Dinah Craik, (died 1887) a prolific and very popular author, wrote a novel in 1859 entitled *A Life For a Life*, which centred around a woman who had a child out of wedlock.

Late in life Craik wrote a little-known short piece of fiction called *King Arthur* (1886) which addresses issues such as child abuse, and also makes the case for legal adoption which at that point in England and Wales, was still 30 years away. She even adopted a baby girl who had been abandoned at the age of nine months on the roadside, and who had been taken to the workhouse to face an uncertain future. Other authors who wrote about adoption included George Eliot (*Silas Marner*), Charles Dickens (*Bleak House*; *Great Expectations*), Elizabeth Barrett Browning (*Aurora Leigh*), Charlotte Yonge (*Hope and Fears*), and Emily Bronte (*Wuthering Heights*).

Wilkie Collins did not write about adoption, but he did have a reputation for writing in a way that supported the causes of women, and his works included the play *The New Magdalene*, in which the heroine is a reformed fallen woman, and the novel *Fallen Leaves*, in which a man marries a reformed fallen woman and has to suffer the social consequences of his devotion to her. Many other playwrights included characters who were fallen women, but not many of them included a fallen woman with a child.

Adoption was also a popular story to be told in serial form or as a short story in magazines, including those with a religious message. One such story, *Her Children by Adoption*, by Sarson C.J. Ingham and published in *Quiver* Magazine in January 1885, tells the tale of a newly 'released' (that is, she has just left her employment) governess who has been left a house and money in trust, which allows her to live on her own means and in comfort. However, feeling something was lacking in her life, she was inspired by a talk given to her ladies group by the 'father' of a children's home to consider adopting a child.

First, she lays down conditions. 'If I had not a gentle, refined character to deal with, the plan might not work happily ... I want only good material to work upon.' The proprietor of the children's home reassures her, saying 'I will not knowingly burden you with any likely candidate for a hospital or a lunatic-asylum', and happily was able to provide two young sisters of well-born but feckless family. Naturally, the story has a happy ending, with the children growing into loving, intelligent and healthy young women, and overall the story is a splendid advertisement for the idea of adoption, especially to the devout readership of the magazine who may wish to 'save' a child.

Plays and songs also used the notion of adoption for entertainment – in the journal *The Ladies Monthly Museum* in 1821, the play *The Miller's Maid* is reviewed, and in the review it describes 'scenes laid in humble life' and declares, 'no high born personages are introduced or even hinted at'. It included two characters who were 'children of adoption', one being in the care of a miller, and the other being a foundling in the care of a soldier. The review emphasises the fact that the play concentrates solely on the 'feelings and sensibilities of the poor', and it is interesting that the 'melodrama' links adoption and poverty in this way – presumably because it is something that the audience can readily recognise.

Institutions
The idea of an institution for displaced children – foundlings, illegitimate, orphans, or simply unwanted – was not new by the nineteenth century. Thomas Coram's Foundling Hospital had been established in 1741, as a result of the horror Coram felt on observing the many abandoned babies in the streets of London. Taking predominantly infants up to the age of 12 months, the Hospital tried hard to look after the children it took in, and some years later expanded its remit to include children from other areas, although this led to an unfortunate trade in child transportation with unscrupulous vagrants taking money to transport infants to the Hospital with very little care given along the way.

In 1869, the Children's Home was founded, which always undertook adoptions where it was safe to do so. The founder, Thomas Bowman Stephenson, was another passionate redeemer of children who had been terribly affected by the plight of London's street children. He aimed to create a family style home for his young charges which was as different to the workhouse as it was possible to achieve – the ambience was to be loving but disciplined, with a master or matron for each home-style 'family' unit. From the late 1870s young women – some of them orphans who had been originally taken in by the home – enrolled on ground-breaking childcare courses run by the Home and became 'Sisters of the Children', going on to work in the homes full-time. Branches of the society spread quickly and in 1908 the name was changed to the National Children's Home and Orphanage.

By the end of the nineteenth century there was a bewildering array of institutions, especially in the cities, that could take in a child or a woman in distress. In the Gore's Directory of Liverpool and Birkenhead for 1900, there is an impressive total of 27 institutions listed to cater for 'displaced children' and their mothers, which includes: Waifs and Strays; Canon Lister's Boys Homes; Barnardos; Home for Waifs and Strays; Home for Destitute Children; Liverpool Wesleyan Mission Girls Home; Ellen Cliff Home for Fallen Women; The Home (for fallen women); the NSPCC.

This long list also includes the Medina Home for Children, the only one in the directory which specifically stated it would take children born out of wedlock: 'This institution receives illegitimate, destitute and orphan children, and assists young girls who have made the first slip from virtue to obtain situations and thus have an opportunity to retrieve their character and once more to return to the path of virtue and respectability.' Of course, it was not the only institution to take in illegitimate children and their 'fallen' mothers, but it was the only one to proclaim it loud and clear. Otherwise, it was a fairly conservative organisation in that it educated and trained 'the boys as artisans and the girls as domestic servants'.

These institutions often contained several hundred children and while they may have looked like magnificent pieces of public architecture and a credit to the city fathers who encouraged them, they cannot have been even remotely like a home from home to the children living in them. Yet they were symbolic of the view that these children were a 'problem' group who should be dealt with collectively, as if dealing with them on a wholesale scale would eliminate the problem more swiftly.

A perfect example of such an orphanage is the Mount Pleasant District Orphan Asylum in Liverpool. Listed in the 1901 Census the Master of the Asylum ('asylum' was a word used for numerous kinds of institution and not just those housing lunatics) was one George Williams from Surrey. His wife was the matron, and there were nine 'officers' who included school masters, sub-matrons, and a sewing mistress, and sixteen live-in female servants, who included a nurse, cook, seamstress and laundress.

This live-in team, no doubt supported by day cleaners and other staff who did not live in, supported 242 boys and girls aged from two months to sixteen years, although the majority of the children (205) were aged between nine and sixteen years. Out of all these children, the majority were born in Liverpool, with only seventeen recorded as being born elsewhere, although in institutions of this kind care was not always taken to be accurate in the recording of such data. On the surface, the ratio of staff to children was good – one member of staff to eight children – but this includes all staff including the servants, so individual attention must have been rare for the children.

It is also not easy to ascertain how many of these children would have had the potential to be adopted out, but if the later trend during adoptions in the twentieth century is any indicator, very few of the children older than about six years could have looked forward to having a new family. This would mean that unless someone wanted an older child for a specific reason – and taking an older child to use for work or to tend members of the family was deeply frowned upon – these children would be long-term residents of the asylum. The best they could hope for would be to concentrate on their training as domestic servants or tradesmen, so that they could make their own way in the world and not end up, as adults, in the workhouse.

Another institution which took in 'fallen women' and their babies was the House of Providence Home for Desolate Women, also in Liverpool. Opened in 1891 by Monsignor James Nugent, a much loved social campaigner, especially for children, the home was a haven for fallen women who had just had their first – and hopefully only – illegitimate baby. The Monsignor was another activist who thought 'first timers' had a better chance of being redeemed than habitual offenders. In December 1900, in an impassioned but rather florid letter to the *Liverpool Mercury*, Monsignor Nugent said:

> *Amid the joyous surroundings of the great festival* [Christmas] *there comes the wail of many heart- broken and destitute fellow creatures ... none more utterly desolate than the poor unfortunate females, who, through circumstances of misplaced confidence or otherwise, has become a mother, and finds herself basely deceived and cruelly deserted, with a helpless infant to provide for. So many ... seek to end their trouble by resorting to child murder and suicide. Spurned by their partners in guilt, and ostracised by their own kith and kin ... Help me to save them from despair and ruin! They can be rescued if we but stretch forth a helping hand.*

Monsignor Nugent goes on to describe his home:

> *The House of Providence, at West Dingle, Liverpool, affords a safe refuge for these neglected and forlorn ones, and at present over 40 unwedded mothers, with their helpless babes, find that shelter and protection ... denied them by outraged friends and society ... poor ruined girls, left alone in the World, penniless,*

without home or friends, out on the streets, starving in the midst of plenty.

Finally, this tireless campaigner makes his appeal for donations:

Help me to rescue them from the perils to which they are exposed ... the cry of these forsaken and deserted creatures, mingling with the mute entreaty of their hapless babes, must surely reach every Christian and compassionate heart ... spare at least a little to help forward this great work for the rescue of the fallen. Any contributions of old clothing, &co, or materials from which garments can be made, would be very acceptable.

The *Tablet* journal of November 1899 also described the building's 'lofty and capacious dormitory' and 'well appointed nursery'. Between 1897 and 1905, the home supported over 200 women and their babies, and when the campaigning priest died in 1907, a statue was erected in his honour, which among other accolades, described the Monsignor as a 'Saviour of Fallen Womanhood'.

Fallen women were not just supported within an institution. Once they had shown suitable contrition and given every indication that this first 'fall' would be the only one, as at the Medina Home, they would be helped while living in the community, either with, or preferably without, their baby. While they attempted to rebuild their life with gainful employment, enthusiastic lady social welfare workers would keep an eye on them, as Plate 2 shows.

In this lantern slide from a set used to illustrate the work of an unknown social welfare organisation in London in about 1900, the fallen woman, looking gaunt and desperate, sits with Bible in hand awaiting the arrival of her welfare worker. On this occasion the miscreant is twice fallen – 'twice she fell, but twice in penitence she was restored', and as such, this young woman is one of the lucky ones to have been given another chance. One would imagine that this was part of a set to encourage donations for a campaign, as to be able to 'save' a twice fallen woman shows an additional level of commitment and higher levels of success.

Of course, the House of Providence only took responsibility for mothers and babies; what of the babies and children who were not with their parents, who had been abandoned, or who had to be given up by their family? In the nineteenth century and into the twentieth century, the orphanage was an obvious solution. The Cherry Tree Orphanage in Sheffield occupied seven acres of land on the outskirts of town and could accommodate seventy children, as stated in the *Kelly's Directory* of 1881, 'of all denominations and from all parts of the British Empire'. Boys and girls from the age of five years were admitted. They were educated to a basic standard and the girls were trained to become domestic servants.

Not many orphanages could boast the glamour of the world of theatre, however. The Actors' Orphanage was first begun in the 1890s as the Actors' Orphanage Fund, and from the start it had eminent sponsors such as the famous actor Sir Henry Irving, who recruited the Princess Royal and the Princess of Wales as patrons. In 1906, the Fund opened its first orphanage building in Croydon, the primary interest being to 'board, clothe and educate destitute children of actors and actresses, and fit them for useful positions in after life'. This not only included children who were true orphans, but also those who had parents who were unable to support them due to, for example, physical or mental incapacity.

As well as looking after children within the institution, the orphanage sometimes adopted children out or placed them with a foster parent; on occasion they also left a delicate child with her/his mother and supported them on an outreach basis. The orphanage supporters were adept at fund raising, one of their most popular and successful methods being the annual garden party instigated in 1906. (Plate 5 shows an advert for a garden party which took place in around 1920, a worthwhile fund raiser for many years.)

When it came to the everyday care of the children there were some rocky moments, with the food, education and supervision of the children called into question, but efforts were made to resolve these and the children left the orphanage ready to work as domestic servants, if girls (some even made it to teacher training), or as gardeners or manual workers, if boys. A few even went into the theatre, hardly surprising given the origins of the orphanage.

The original Actors' Orphanage occupied two large Victorian houses in Croydon and provided accommodation on a smaller, more homely scale. However, not that far away was the Reedham Orphanage in Purley, Surrey (originally known as the Asylum for Fatherless Children), which could take approximately 300 children from the age of three months to eleven years. This building hardly represents accommodation on a homely scale; the image on Plate 3, from the *Illustrated London News* of July 1894, shows this 'stately and commodious building', as it was enthusiastically described in the accompanying article, 'which stands with its chapel, its sanatorium, the surrounding playgrounds and swimming-bath', all of which could be enjoyed in the 'hardy, breezy air' of Reedham.

Inside, we are told that the resident staff 'do all that can be done by careful kindness and good management for the welfare, in mind and body, and for the morals and manners, as well as the intellectual culture of their young charges'. This meant, in reality, the usual routine of an orphanage – housewifery lessons for the girls and carpentry or similar for the boys – in other words, training for a life of useful service. Plate 4 shows girls learning the skills of good laundering, although this is clearly an idealised picture of what such a room would really look like.

The orphanage was in the news at this time because of the high-profile visitor to its summer festival – Her Royal Highness the Duchess of Teck, who handed out the school prizes and watched the girls and infants do musical drill and the boys carry out athletic exercises, battalion drill and swimming. This was another orphanage which was non-denominational and it was there strictly to 'receive and bless the fatherless infant' and to raise her or him using scriptural principles and precepts but with no adherence to a particular denomination beyond that.

From its foundation, it took in children regardless of 'sex, place or religious connection', but like many such institutions it did not provide any further specifications. While most of them took in illegitimate children, it would not be something that they would necessarily advertise – why would they, when some commentators might see that as the harbouring of 'bad blood'?

There was one institution which was not a place for the 'displaced' child to go, however. In 1913 the Mental Deficiency Act gave local authorities the power to certify destitute pregnant women or those judged as 'immoral' and detain them indefinitely in mental institutions. Known as 'The Eugenicist's Bill', it was the ultimate legislative link between immorality and imbecility and included a category of 'moral imbecile' – a person who displayed mental weakness coupled with strong vicious or criminal tendencies and on whom punishment has little deterrent effect. Women detained under the Act were regarded as incapable of controlling their sexual inclinations, and also vulnerable to exploitation from men. It seems that the original move to include a category of the 'sexually feeble minded' for such women was unnecessary; women informally labelled in this way were detained anyway. Their illegitimate children would have been housed in a separate institution, such as an orphanage, or quietly absorbed into their birth family, whilst their mother languished in the asylum a victim of her 'unacceptable' conduct.

Charitable and Campaigning Organisations
The end of the nineteenth century also saw the inception of many campaigning and charitable movements. One of the most famous and long lived (indeed, it is still in operation today as The Children's Society) was the Church of England Waifs and Strays Society. It was founded in 1881 by Edward de Montjoie Rudolf for boys and girls and was funded by contributions from Poor Law Unions, from individuals who sponsored particular children, and from other forms of fundraising – over the decades the society became adept at a gentle form of publicity, based more on fundraising than on blatant requests for foster and adoptive parents to come forward. It also, of course, received considerable support from the Church of England.

The society started its activities in London, pro-actively seeking out destitute and homeless children. By 1896 it had 2,300 children in its care, 700 of whom were in foster care, and it also maintained dozens of homes for the children who were not fostered. The homes were preferably established in out-of-town settings and the ambience was to be, as far as possible, a home not an institution (along the lines of the cottages homes in Plate 4), and a good Christian and loving home at that. From these homes the children would attend a church school for preference, or if that was not available, the local community school. Each home had a matron or master, and training or instruction was based on reward rather than punishment, although there was a sliding scale of punishments which included physical discipline as well as sanctions, such as missed meals.

As was the case with many such organisations, the children were schooled, but also prepared for a life of useful work. The girls were almost always trained to become domestic servants, and stayed on at the home for two years after finishing school in order to learn 'housewifery'. Some local benefactors even allowed the girls into their homes as 'pupil servants' so they could learn to be more than a household drudge, thereby enhancing their employment prospects.

Happily for some of the foster children, they were adopted by their foster parents who voluntarily gave up their boarding out fee (a maximum of 5d a week) from the society to have the child for their own – this was beneficial for the child, who then had a family of their own, but also for the society who had one less fee to pay out. As one of the instructional manuals for the employees of Waifs and Strays says, 'Not only is a real home provided for the little ones, but also a mother's love ... The cheerless and monotonous life of a childless woman has been brightened, and pent up sympathies have at last found the object which has been long sought for.'

For would-be foster parents there was a application form to complete. This asked questions about their income, enquired if the applicant was a communicant of the Church of England, and requested information about other family members in the house including children, and so on. Those who were related to the child, or in receipt of poor relief, were not accepted, and no foster parent could take in more than four children from the society. The accommodation had to be 'decent' and the children were not to sleep in the same room as an adult, and for children over the age of seven, they must not sleep in the same room as a married couple.

Foster parents who did go a step further and adopt their young charge had to complete more forms, and the birth parents also had to do this, in an attempt to make the adoption as irreversible as possible – it had no legal foundation at this time. Sadly, in a few cases, birth relatives did come forward to claim the child back, which although probably not always in the best interests of a settled and much loved adopted child, the birth family had every right to do. As a deterrent, the society included in the agreement a sanction whereby if the birth family took the child back after the adoption, they would have to pay up to £13 towards the expenses of the society – the equivalent of approximately £4,700 today.

For children who stayed in the homes, it was policy to keep in touch with the young people after they left, in order to keep them on the right path, while for foster children, a local clergyman or the 'ladies of the neighbourhood' were to supervise the placement and ensure a high standard of care for the boarded out children. The Waifs and Strays Emigration Committee also worked to establish 'distributing homes' in Canada, so that children could be sent abroad to start their lives again there.

The Case Committee decided which children the Waifs and Strays should take in, and divided children into various categories, such as orphans, the cruelly treated, deserted children and illegitimate children. With this last group, the idea was to take in the illegitimate child to allow the mother an opportunity to redeem herself by giving her the freedom to resume work. However, the society insisted upon a regular payment of 4d per week for the maintenance of the child, and if the payments ceased, it was expected that the child would be taken back by the mother. The reason for this was, it was said, that the society did not want to be seen as making it easy for a mother to 'get rid of' her child, then promptly go off and have another illegitimate baby, in which case Waifs and Strays would be 'offering a premium to sin'. They also strongly encouraged the mother to pursue the father of the baby for maintenance payments.

All organisations need funds, of course, and apart from their major institutional funding, local workers were strongly encouraged to help with fund raising. This was a mixture of bazaars and sales of work, magazine subscriptions, collections, Lantern Lectures with an entry fee, and 'Pound Days' – as a novel way of encouraging donations, well-wishers could give any item such as food or cloth to make outfits for the children, up 16oz or 1lb (slightly under half a kilo) in weight, possibly so that people who could not afford to give money could still support the cause. The society took its work very seriously indeed, seemed well organised and committed, and was acutely aware of the moral work it was doing – and it would seem that many of its workers and foster parents regarded their contribution as a vocation and not just an everyday way of supporting a charity.

The Salvation Army was formed in 1865, and although it was primarily concerned to keep mothers and their babies together rather than separating them so that the child could be adopted, their child welfare work was wide-ranging. In 1885, they were involved in the famous and luridly reported case of the abduction and sale of Eliza Armstrong. Eliza was sold by her alcoholic mother for £5 (the rough equivalent of £2,000 today) to one Rebecca Jarrett, who was secretly working for W.T. Stead, the zealous campaigning proprietor of the tabloid-style journal, *The Pall Mall Gazette*, and for Bramwell Booth, then the Salvation Army's Chief of Staff. The whole transaction had been set up to highlight the trafficking and abuse of underage girls and Eliza was later taken to a place of safety relatively unharmed. Partly as a result of the case, the Criminal Law Amendment Act was passed and the age of consent raised to 16 years.

W.T. Stead was to continue with his somewhat maverick endeavours to help disadvantaged children. In 1890, he co-founded the journal, *The Review of Reviews*, which he used to promote advertisements for his other new venture, 'The Baby Exchange'. Despite the extraordinary name of his venture, which makes it sound like more of a child 'library', it aimed to be a serious and genuine adoption agency.

Some of the advertisements are given below:

Children Offered for Adoption.
Applicants must write to me at the office of the
Review of Reviews.
A boy, one year and nine months old. Fair, with flaxen hair; a
nice healthy little fellow. Illegitimate.

A baby boy. A year old. Of gentle birth. Deserted by its father.

A father, whose profession obliges him to move about
constantly, would like both or one of his motherless girls
adopted. Ages eleven and seven.

A married woman, whose husband has deserted her and her
children, would be thankful to have her baby girl adopted.

A boy, aged six. His mother is dead. Has a bad stepfather.

A boy, his mother died when he was one month old. No
relatives able to help. Father alive, but in very poor
circumstances; wishes to keep out of the workhouse.

Boy. Born November 1894. Ireland.

Girl. Born September, 1895. Southsea. Fine healthy child.
Mother dead. Father gone to Africa. Married second time.
Left the child on the hands of a friend, who would gladly
have her adopted.

A HISTORY OF ADOPTION

Girl. Born May, 1894. Hampshire. Mother will give up all claims.
Father deserted his family.

A baby boy. Illegitimate. About three months old. Fair child.
Its mother is a lady.

A girl, eleven years of age. Half French. Speaks French, Spanish and
English. Is neither pretty nor plain. Her mother is alive, but very poor.

A boy of seven years of age, a nice child. Illegitimate.

Stead also published the details of more than 55 couples registered
with his Baby Exchange who wished to adopt a child:

> *A lady and gentleman in good standing in society wish to adopt*
> *a baby boy of gentle birth, the child if possible of well educated*
> *parents in their own position in life. Age preferred between ten*
> *and twelve months. He must be certified by the adopter's own*
> *doctor as healthy, with if possible a good hereditary record. Must*
> *be intelligent, with a well shaped head. The boy when adopted*
> *will be adopted outright. Nor will any of his relations know*
> *where he is or into whose family he has been received. He will*
> *be brought up as an English gentleman, well educated and*
> *provided for, with good prospects when he grows up.*

W.T. Stead added to following postscript to the above notice:

> *As both the lady and gentleman are personally known to me, and*
> *as they have no family of their own, although they are*
> *passionately fond of children, I shall be very glad if any readers*
> *who may know of a suitable baby boy will communicate with*
> *me. It is not indispensable that it should be legitimate, but the*
> *circumstances of its illegitimacy will be closely inquired into.*

Reading the above notice from a modern cultural perspective makes
it seem rather at odds with what we might see now as the reasons for
adopting. Parents today adopt for many reasons but high on the list would
be to want to love a child as their own and do their best by her or him.

64

Nowhere in this notice does the concept of love appear, rather it concentrates more on a clinical description of what the child should look like and what his background is. It smacks of eugenics to talk about a 'well shaped head' and a 'good hereditary record'.

However, the warning that the birth family will be excluded completely is understandable, bearing in mind that the adoption would be a private arrangement, and as there are no officially sanctioned public bodies at this time to support the couple with their choice of baby, other than the eccentric and impassioned Mr Stead, their caution was probably wise and was intended to prevent the birth family coming forward at a later date (often once the child attained working age) to reclaim their offspring. Nothing could be done about this as the arrangement was not legally enforceable, other than to keep the birth family at as far a distance as was possible.

The Baby Exchange is not unusual for its time either, in that it is one of many organisations started and operated by totally untrained individuals, who acted for the best of motives, which may or may not have been in the best interests of the child. It is not known if there were any follow-up investigations to see if any of the children whose adoption was arranged via the Baby Exchange were doing well in their new families, but this is unlikely. Many such organisations at this time saw the solution to the problem of the child without a family to begin and end with the fact of the adoption; it was as if the child would be remade anew in the image of the new family and any previous problems would be wiped from the slate.

Baby Exchanges were not necessary for many people who wished to adopt a child, but by adopting and, in particular, in trying to conceal the fact of the adoption, respectable couples could find themselves in court for the first time in their lives. At the end of 1891, a young man named Lambert in Holbeck, Leeds, advertised for a baby to adopt, and in response, one Annie Kendall and another woman called on him and his wife, Lily, at their home. Annie told them she had just had a baby and would be willing for them to adopt it.

Subsequently, a prosperous looking man also called on the Lamberts and asked if they would register the child as theirs – presumably an attempt to conceal the disgrace Annie had brought on her family and to cut all ties with the child. The Lamberts, who assumed the man was the father of the baby (who was two weeks old when they 'adopted' it), were reassured by the man's self-assurance and proceeded to have the baby registered as their own, which they must have thought gave them extra security as his parents too. However, in doing so, the delighted new adoptive mother had broken the law in giving false information to the registrar, was found out and ended up being fined £1 to cover costs.

It was said in the Lamberts' defence that they were eminently respectable people, childless and simply desperate for a child to call their own, even though Mr Lambert was out of work at the time. The magistrate who presided over the case in January 1892 was clearly sympathetic to the Lamberts and their desire to have a family, and expressed regret that the man who had so ill-advised them could not be prosecuted, as he was more at fault than the new parents were. As to whether this was disapproval of the 'disposing' of a birth child to adoption, or encouraging a breach of the law, it is difficult now to say.

'Boarding Out' and Other Solutions
In the 1880s and the years following, there were a number of significant developments. In 1886 the Guardianship of Infants Act established that on the death of the father of an infant, the mother alone was to be the guardian unless the father had appointed a guardian, in which case a joint arrangement applied between mother and guardian. Overall, a court could override the Common Law rights of the father in relation to the custody of his infant children. This is significant as here is a widow being given rights to have her child despite being a single mother at that point.

The 1889 Poor Law Act empowered Poor Law Guardians to 'adopt' children in their care, which meant in practice that they assumed parental rights and responsibilities over a child until he or she reached the age of 18. At first it applied only to deserted children, but this widened later in 1899 with another Poor Law Act, to include orphans and the children of disabled parents or those deemed to have impaired judgement or to be unfit to have control of children. Because of the broad parameters used, only a small proportion of these children were illegitimate. It proved to be a useful tool for the Guardians to have, and by 1908 12,417 children had been 'adopted' in this way.

One example of the use of this power occurred in 1913, when the five children of Frederick Battelly and his wife, of Islington in London, were adopted by the local Board of Guardians. Battelly (he claimed) had left his wife and children to go in search of work and that they had to go into the workhouse as they could not manage. At this point, the children were adopted, so when he returned from his wanderings and tried to claim his children back, saying he could now make a home for them, it was too late – he was informed in no uncertain terms that they were no longer his children. He appealed against the adoption, but this was an unwise decision as at the North London Police Court, evidence was put forward by the Guardians that the Battelly family had repeatedly been in receipt of poor relief, and that Mrs Battelly had been convicted three times for drunkenness.

Accordingly, the adoption remained in place due to the unstable home background the children had previously endured and the unfit nature of the parents, and a week later, Battelly's woes were compounded when the Guardians attempted to extract maintenance payments from him for his children. This failed on a legal technicality, for which he was no doubt very thankful.

Some commentators wanted official intervention to be taken further. In a radical article written for the journal *The Fortnightly Review* by Emma Samuels, the Government was strongly urged to adopt the nation's 'street Arabs' (children who lived on the streets) and train them for essential trades and for entry into the armed forces. Of these children, the writer says, 'Their birth a curse to those who have been its cause; their education one of oaths and blows; their future the workhouse and prison; half naked, half starved, subjected to every possible suffering and temptation, dedicated from their cradle to a life of crime.'

The article goes on to praise the recent legislation that had benefited most children, and it enthuses about the work of the relatively new organisation the National Society for the Prevention of Cruelty to Children (NSPCC). Yet, on noting that many children ended up in the workhouse, separated from their parents, it condemns these institutions, saying they may make the child's circumstances even worse than they were on the street in their degradation: 'The influences and surroundings of the poor-house are usually of the worst description, fatal to them in their growing years.' The answer is, we are told, not to make the children enemies of the state in this way, but to have the state adopt them 'and be made its future servants instead of its future enemies'. The method of doing this, and redeeming these street children, was to be as follows:

Why should the state not become the father of the fatherless ...
and properly organise Government refuges, compulsory military
and naval training schools, or training ships for boys, and
compulsory technical training schools for girls, where the
children be made apprentices of the state? ... Let any young child
that is homeless and whose parents or natural guardians have
in the judgement of a court forfeited their right to its custody be
adopted by the State ... When old enough let the boys be drilled
and disciplined as soldier and sailors, and drafted on at a proper
age into our army and ... navy. Let such as are physically unfit
for these services be trained to handicrafts or agricultural
employments. Let the girls be trained and disciplined as
domestic and farm servants. Numbers (of girls and unfit boys)
could be apprenticed out in rural districts among cottagers on
the family system ... which often leads to the adoption of the child
and its final absorption into the family.

The institutions where the children lived while training would be 'self maintaining child communities', with the residents doing all maintenance and domestic work, and 'When the boys and girls have attained a mature age, it would be possible to provide for the emigration of selected groups trained to different trades ... which could be planted as communities in different parts of the vast unoccupied tracts of the Empire.' In the opinion of the author of the article, it was time to lift these children from the streets, make them the 'property' of the state, and make them a credit to the nation.

The opinions of Emma Samuels reflect some of the activities that charitable organisations and the Board of Guardians were endeavouring to put into practice already, as she readily acknowledges. But the idea that the state should become a 'parent' to the children, which at that time would mean it had absolute control over the fate of them – and full responsibility – was radical.

It is unlikely, however, that the state would want to undertake such a huge task and it was surely no substitute for what these children had apparently always lacked – a family and a home of their own. The very reason why many charities such as Dr Barnardo's switched eventually to the cottage style or homestead accommodation for small groups of children was that they realised that what the children – many of them traumatised by their early lives – needed was exactly that family ambience, not to become a part of a 'factory' producing useful drones for Imperial expansion. On the other hand, late Victorian society was used to the concept of using children's labour, so it would have seemed a reasonable argument to many.

At the same time, the NSPCC was forging a place for itself as a key player in the campaign against cruelty to children. It had been founded under its most familiar name in 1889 following more localised beginnings in Liverpool and across London from 1883 onwards. Once again, a children's aid organisation had impressive support, with none other than Queen Victoria as patron. By 1910, it had 250 inspectors (who were known colloquially as 'The Cruelty Man') dealing with over 50,000 complaints, armed with power as an 'authorised person' (thanks to the 1904 Prevention of Cruelty Act) to remove children from homes where they were being neglected or cruelly treated, once the sanction of a Justice of the Peace had been obtained.

The graphic photographs used by the NSPCC to illustrate the appalling state some children were in at the time of rescue, are painful to view today and would have been equally shocking to people at the time, but they had the desired effect of making the charity high profile and successful in conveying its message – that the neglect and abuse of children must be stopped. It was partly thanks to a display of such photographs that a sequence of events began which led to the arrest and conviction of Amelia Dyer, the notorious baby farmer.

At about the same time, the Salvation Army was involved in the rescue – and sometimes the adoption – of destitute children. It started an Adoption Book to record these events, and one of the earliest entries was for Miss Emma Booth, daughter of the Army's founder, William Booth – she adopted a son as an example to others. An Adoption Department, with its own board, was set up, and over the years they continued to improve their adoption procedures. The adoptive family had to be Salvationists and the Army tended to concentrate on the adoption of older children at first. This was not the only way in which they helped single mothers – they also did their best to support the mother in keeping her child if she could, on the grounds that keeping mother and child together would help the mother turn her life around and live to a higher moral standard.

Eighteen-eighty-nine was an important year for children in other ways, as were the few years following. In that year, the Prevention of

Cruelty to, and Protection of Children Act was passed, which made ill-treatment, neglect of or causing of suffering to children punishable, and it also prohibited begging by boys under the age of 14, and girls under the age of 16. At last, the state was intervening; warrants could be issued for authorities to enter the homes of children thought to be at risk, and arrests could be made of those inflicting harm upon children.

In 1891, the Custody of Children Act enabled courts to prevent the return of children who were staying with friends or relatives to parents who were deemed to be unfit. It also prevented parents from 'reclaiming' children when they reached working age, a clear attempt to limit the economic exploitation of children by their families, and an emphasis that to house and feed a child was not enough: how they were treated, and what the children did with their days, was now a matter of wider concern.

Another way to get poor children out of the Poor Law System and into family homes was to use a practice known as 'boarding out'. This was sanctioned by the English Poor Law Board in 1870 and was essentially a way of fostering out poor children to family homes, albeit those of the labouring classes only. The reasons for doing it were straightforward – it was an attempt to get the children out of the workhouses and the bad influences which might be lurking there. It was also hoped that the children would experience what it was like to have security and the affection of a family, which no matter how caring the workhouse staff tried to be, was extremely difficult to replicate in such a large institution.

It was also an attempt to ensure that pauper girls had an opportunity to escape what were seen as the immoral influences of being in a workhouse, and to give them a chance to learn how to be good housewives, and more importantly, good domestic servants so that they would have gainful and respectable employment when older – a system sometimes referred to as 'home training'. An editorial in the *Montgomeryshire Express and Radnor Times* put the case for boarding out in eloquent terms:

> *Every thoughtful individual is agreed that the orphan, the outcast, or otherwise, unbefriended, helpless child, should have a home outside the pauper citadel, where it is not only branded with the ugly stamp of pauperism, but reared in sight of, if not in actual association with, much that is ... vicious and depraved*

in human nature ... The kindest and the best of the workhouse masters and matrons cannot fulfil the part of foster father and mother to individual children, nor create that wholesome atmosphere which they require during those impressive years ... A home, which means the love and care of parent or guardian personally bestowed, is essential to the development of the whole nature ... We hope to see a day when, instead of being herded into huge depots for human wreckage, these children will be boarded out with respectable people, and thus permitted to enjoy the helpful associations of family life.

The new system of dealing with pauper children had both detractors and supporters. An article in the *Merthyr Telegraph and General Advertiser* of 16 February 1877 reported:

The National Committee for boarding out pauper children ... report that the system of home training, as distinguished from massing children together in large numbers, is gaining favour among guardians of the poor. Statistics are given in the report shewing that children in some of the Metropolitan district schools (institutions) cost £36 a year each, while boarded-out children cost only about 4s a week (£17 per year), and in addition to the visits of the inspectors, the foster parents are seen periodically by committees who undertake to watch over the children.

It would seem that along with the laudable reasons of moral and domestic improvement, the temptation of looking after the children more economically could not be resisted; in addition, some workhouses also used the space freed up by boarding out children to house 'harmless lunatics' and 'imbeciles' who would then not take up valuable space in the county asylums.

It was even suggested by a speaker at the conference of the Women Guardians and Local Government Association in Manchester in 1905 that boarding out was a way of overcoming the 'evils of heredity' in these pauper children – in other words, to sublimate the 'bad blood' that children from these unfortunate backgrounds inherited – and of course, many of them would be illegitimate with mothers regarded as morally bankrupt. At the same conference, warnings were given about the choice of foster parents for these already vulnerable children. Solemn advice was given that the children should be dressed in flannelette and their teeth carefully attended to, while any child whose life was found to have been insured by the foster parent should be removed to a place of safety immediately. Unfortunately, these warnings and advice were not always heeded.

In November 1884, in Retford, the death of an 11-year-old boarded out boy named George Hind made the news. Young George and his older sister had been placed by the Board of Guardians about 14 months before with a Henry and Annie Ward, who were paid 3s. a week for having each of the children, plus 10s a quarter for clothing and school fees. George was in delicate health and was lame with poor feet, but it would appear that his clothing allowance was not being used for his benefit, as witnesses came forward to say that he had been seen wearing ill-fitting and inadequate clothes, with no coat on bitterly cold days.

He was often in tears and complained to numerous people of the cold and his great hunger and was compelled to do heavy chores such as vegetable gardening and carrying several buckets of water when his health was not up to the job. Once he had grown the vegetables, he had to go round the local shops trying to sell the produce. George's foster mother had been seen to beat him with a shovel and his foster father was physically abusive too. George eventually died from tubercular meningitis, but at his inquest the jury 'found as a fact that the deceased had been systematically ill-treated, and that such ill-treatment accelerated death, and that therefore the foster parents were deserving of the severest censure'. It was not reported what happened to George's sister, although one hopes she was swiftly removed from this cruel and abusive household.

Despite the best efforts of the Poor Relief System and an enthusiastic network of lady inspectors (it was proclaimed that inspections of children must be the work of women with their motherly attributes), boarding out poor children was not proving to be any better a solution to the problem of children without homes, than any other on offer. It is perhaps due to the uncertainties of boarding out that even by the beginning of the twentieth century, less than 4 per cent of all English and Welsh children in receipt of some form of public relief had been placed with foster parents.

It stands to reason that if the Poor Law Guardians had taken over the role of parent in some cases, they then had the right to allow or refuse to have the child adopted out to another person or family, and some private adoptions did occur in this period, long before the legalised adoptions after 1926. One such adoption occurred in 1915, just one year into the First World War. On 12 June in that year, William and Elizabeth Williams of Harlech in North Wales signed an adoption agreement to undertake the upbringing of a child named Cassie Davies, the orphan child of Hugh and Ann Davies.

Cassie had been born in 1901 in Glamorganshire and was 13 years old at the time of the adoption. After Cassie was orphaned, she became the responsibility of the Guardians of the Poor of the Bridgend and Cowbridge Union, Glamorganshire, and therefore it was they who agreed to 'deliver', as the adoption agreement says, the young Cassie to Mr and Mrs Williams. In return, Cassie's new parents had to accept certain conditions. Firstly and obviously, they had to agree to 'adopt the said child, and to maintain, support and educate her in a proper and suitable manner'. Mr and Mrs Williams rather curiously had to hand over 1s. to the trustees and in return 'the said trustees (Guardians) hereby grant and assign to the parties of the second part, all their rights to the possession, custody and control of the said child, and all right, profit and advantage to be derived from the custody and possession of the said child'.

So far, so good, except that to the average modern parent, the idea of having rights to profit, advantage or have 'possession' of a child seems rather archaic and uncomfortably reminiscent of earlier Victorian notions of the child as a commodity.

Mr and Mrs Williams also had to agree to:

board, lodge, clothe and educate the child in a manner suitable to the station of the (new parents) ... in the same manner as if the said Cassie Davies was their own lawful child ... They will ... provide the said child with all the necessaries and discharge all debts and liabilities which the said child may incur for necessaries and will indemnify the said trustees against all actions, claims and demands in respect thereof: and that they will bring up the said child and cause her to be instructed in the principles of the Baptist Denomination.

73

The final part of the agreement is an assurance from the trustees (Guardians) that they will not in any way 'interfere with or in any way disturb' the newly bestowed parental rights of Cassie's new mother and father, so long as they 'faithfully perform their part to this agreement'. A copy of the agreement was sent to the Board of Guardians of the Conway Union, presumably so that their North Wales colleagues were kept fully informed of the event.

There is a twist to this story in connection with Cassie's earlier life. In the 1911 census, little nine-year-old Cassie is listed as living with her three sisters, Maggie, Annie and Gwennie, but the head of the household is their aunt, one Mary Williams. Mary was born in Dyffryn in Merionethshire which is the county that Cassie eventually moved to after her adoption – and not far from where Mr and Mrs Williams lived. Were William and Elizabeth Williams related to Cassie and Mary?

It was not uncommon for family members to take in children from other relatives who could no longer cope or where the child had been orphaned, and absorb them into their own family group. Possibly in the close-knit culture of rural and sparsely populated Mid Wales, the Williamses were friends of the family and wanted to help out. Whatever the reason, given their address was that of a farm, even if Cassie was much loved and nurtured she would be an extra pair of hands, like any other farmer's daughter. However, the fact that the Guardians were involved meant that Cassie's adoption had to be done formally.

Another example of inter-family 'adoption' occurred in Haslingden, in Lancashire. On the 1911 census, a young couple, Ernest and Betsy Jane Haworth, 21 and 22 years old respectively, are recorded as having been married for two years and with no children. Yet also in the four-roomed house with them is George Collinge Warburton, aged 16, who is listed as an 'adopted boy'. Whose adopted boy is George? It is highly unlikely that such a young couple could have made any formal arrangement for an adoption and of a youth too, not even a child, although George was legally still a minor.

Looking into their background, it transpires that Betsy's unmarried name was Warburton and that as a little girl on the 1891 census, she was living with her father Thomas, her mother Sarah, her maternal grandparents and her sister Amelia. By 1901 Betsy's family circumstances had clearly changed. Now she was living with a 60-year-old man called Fletcher Rawlinson and is described as 'Adopted Daughter'. Listed on the same census, George Warburton is five years old and is in the Haslingden Workhouse as an inmate. It is likely that George is a close relative of Betsy's and she did for George what someone had done for her – gave him a home. More than likely, Betsy had been boarded out by the Board of Guardians and as George was a minor, she was able to apply for the same with George.

At the other end of the scale, in 1914, a bizarre example of child theft occurred in Walthamstow, apparently for the purposes of adoption. At the end of November, a 10-year-old girl called Lucy Carter was playing in the street with her little brother. They were approached by a young woman (later revealed in court to be 22-year-old Florence Powell), who chatted to Lucy and then gave her a penny to buy sweets. Unable to resist the idea of such a treat, Lucy hurried into the shop, the woman having said she would mind the baby while she did. When Lucy came out of the shop, both baby and woman had gone.

Shortly before this abduction, Powell had visited an acquaintance named Annie Snow, and declared 'I have come to adopt your baby ... I am married, and my hubby wants a baby.' Annie refused to sell her baby, but did suggest to Powell that she took her four-year-old son instead! He was rejected for being too old. Powell and one William Elston (charged with receiving the stolen child) ended up in court and the baby was found safe and well, but the case took a bizarre twist when Powell was revealed as having told people she was an aristocrat's daughter – she was nothing of the sort, so it would seem that her fantasies of motherhood were not her only form of make-believe.

Not all thefts and trading in babies was for some form of personal gain. In the spring of 1903, a young married woman named Caroline Carthy in Liswery, near Newport, answered an advertisement appealing for someone to take on a three-week-old baby boy for love only; no money was to be exchanged. She went to meet a Mrs Brown, the midwife who had delivered the baby, and a Miss Davies who was the birth mother. Miss Davies personally put the baby in Caroline's arms and was happy for the adoption to go ahead.

Caroline's husband and the birth mother, a respectable looking young woman of about 30 years of age, signed a document – apparently drawn up by a lawyer – in which the birth mother gave up all rights and claims to the child, and the delighted adoptive parents took their new baby son home. They must have been thrilled to be chosen, as four other people had already come forward to take on the baby but had been rejected.

Tragically, despite what seemed to be relatively respectable beginnings with all care given, the baby did not thrive and died soon after this, despite a doctor being in attendance. The death of the baby prompted an inquest and the coroner raised serious questions about the activities of Mrs Brown, pointing out to her that if she had offered a premium with the baby, he could have ended up in terrible circumstances and in great peril. As it was, the jury noted that Caroline was clearly 'a fond and considerate foster (adoptive) mother' and no harm had been meant to the baby at any point.

It is a shame that this little boy did not live to know the love his adoptive parents clearly had for him, but there would have been hundreds of such arrangements around the country that went unnoticed and unrecorded, of babies and young children who changed hands and went on to live happy lives, doted on by their new families. There is always a mix of circumstance in history, and it is never all bad.

In 1897, the Infant Life Protection Act added to the body of legislation designed to protect privately farmed or fostered children. Henceforward, any foster carer who had in their home children aged under a year old, for more than 24 hours, had to apply for registration. The law was rigorously imposed and the penalties were harsh, even 20 years after the Act came into force. The Children Act of 1908 extended this legislation to include the single fostered child, and gave access for parents to a physician for their child under the Poor Laws if they could not afford a doctor themselves.

Taking out life insurance for children was now prohibited, and farmed or fostered children up to the age of seven were now protected by the law, part of which protection was the compulsory inspection visits of an Infant Life Protection Visitor (ILP). It was now becoming more and more difficult to use baby farming as a route to easy money, and although the new system was not perfect and there were concerns about the insufficient number of ILPs, it was a big step forward in dealing with the problem and it allowed campaigners the space to look at how they were going to approach other child-centred issues, such as child health in general and the mothering skills of the nation's women.

As the twentieth century dawned, the status of children in England and Wales was subtly shifting. At the beginning of the nineteenth century, children were part of a patriarch's domain; they were his and his alone to treat, punish and dispose of as he wished. The state was extremely reluctant to undermine the influence of parents over children and this was considered by some to be positively subversive; where would such intervention end? Would it attack the very foundations of society?

However, taken as a whole, this very society had changed immeasurably in the nineteenth century and the state had to change with it. Over this century, the state had taken over the registration of life events (from July 1837); established a state-run probate system, taking over from the church courts (from 1858); passed legislation to limit the adverse working conditions of women and children, such as the 1833 Factory Act and the Mines and Collieries Act of 1842; and local government in a relatively familiar pattern was established by the Local Governments Act of 1888. The nineteenth century also saw an increasing secularisation of poor relief, and indeed, in most areas, the secular state was becoming ever more important, and ever more visible and intrusive.

In 1880, the Elementary Education Act made education for all children compulsory up to the age of 10 years, which, by 1899, had been raised to 13. At the beginning of the campaign for education for all children, including those of the labouring poor, opposition was based around the argument that such education inhibited a parent's right to bring up a child as they saw fit, and would also encourage a dependence on the state instead of instilling virtues of personal initiative and self-sufficiency.

There was an element of truth to this, as full-time education created a generation of children who were now removed from the world of work and who had become a financial burden on their family – they may be able to do chores at home and part-time work around school hours, but they were not a vital economic unit any more until school days were over at the age of 10.

At the same time, the public dismay and lurid publicity around baby farming had highlighted the plight of illegitimate children or children who did not have a stable family life, and by 1900 many organisations and institutions had sprung up to aid and support children and, in some cases, their lone mothers too. It would be tempting to suggest that children were regarded less as a commodity and were loved and valued more highly, but that might be overstating the progress that had been made.

Alongside these major changes to the way children were perceived and treated in law, were growing calls for a better way of transferring parental responsibilities from a child's birth parents to others, in other words, a more formal way of adopting children. But a precedent was now also set for a close overseeing of the lives of all children, not just with regard to who was their parent, but also over issues of neglect and abuse, malnutrition, education (both moral and academic), housing and family income. The world of the child and their family were be scrutinised and tweaked in an effort to bring the family into modern times in line with the new passion for 'welfare', and the attention was to become ever more intensive.

The First World War

In times of war, inhibitions can waver. With the threat of danger and death looming over most families in Britain between 1914 and 1918, more men and women had affairs, took risks by having sexual relationships before marriage and married in a hurry without going through the usual prolonged courtship. Popular culture reflected this new emotional urgency with songs such as 'I'll Make a Man of You' written and composed by Arthur Wimperis and Herman Finck in 1914 (and famously revived in the movie *Oh What a Lovely War* in 1969).

The lyrics take the point of view of a young woman who is telling the listener exactly how she is going to support the war effort – by encouraging all the nation's girls to only date boys who have joined up: 'On Saturday I'm willing if you'll only take the shilling to make a man of any one of you' (the 'shilling' being the King's shilling given as a token to new recruits to the army). The message is straightforward – use your feminine charms to get a man to join up, and it 'makes you almost proud to be a woman,' and as the chorus suggests, any representative of the forces will do – included in the list is a bosun, rifleman, marine and midshipman!

The message was probably only intended to be a light hearted and mildly risqué encouragement to women to make sure their menfolk joined up, but there must have been thousands of women who bitterly regretted heeding this message when their husbands, boyfriends, fathers and brothers did not come home, especially if using those feminine charms had gone a little further than intended and led to an illegitimate baby. Alongside the more suggestive songs like this, images of chaste mothers, sweethearts and sisters were invoked with songs like 'Keep the Home Fires Burning' (composed by Ivor Novello and Lena Gilbert Ford in 1914), but the notion of keeping the troops happy was no less powerful.

Even Emmeline Pankhurst, who along with her comrades in the

Women's Social and Political Union was previously vilified in the media for their militant campaign to obtain the vote for women, largely abandoned her militant suffrage campaign in order to support the war and strongly encouraged women to join in the war effort by taking up key roles and by urging men to join the armed forces.

The impact on children in general was immense. With their fathers away at the Front and their mothers employed in war work, older children would have had to take on extra responsibility and, at the very least, help out more at home. From a child's point of view they would have missed their fathers, brothers and uncles, been frightened by dire threats of the enemy (some children were threatened with a visit from 'Kaiser Bill' instead of the bogeyman!), and suffered the bereavement of losing family members. Some children in coastal areas and in the South East of England lived with the threat of coastal bombardment or bombing, and food rationing was introduced in February 1918.

With the emphasis so strongly on families pulling together and facing the 'German Peril', as Mrs Pankhurst called it, as one, and putting the soldiers first in all things, it is little wonder that many people embarked on relationships without much prior thought as to the consequences. The result was that newly wed wives also became newly widowed women with young babies to support. The birth rate for babies born outside marriage rose from 4.29 per cent in 1913, to 6.26 per cent in 1918, which looks a small increase, but in statistical and cultural terms it was significant.

Unfortunately, the war could also lead to fraudulent activities in which children were caught up. In September 1915, Elizabeth White of Brixton had a baby, whose father was Robert Abel, a soldier on active service in France. Her baby was stillborn, and if the authorities had known about this, Elizabeth's war separation allowance (a payment made to the dependants of soldiers) would have been stopped.

In order to keep her allowance, Elizabeth advertised for, and obtained a baby – in other words, an informal adoption – and went to register the child as her own. She made the mistake of telling the registrar what she had done and the registrar refused to issue a birth certificate. Subsequently, Elizabeth's mother completed the registration in another area, the adopted baby being given the surname Abel. Elizabeth continued to receive the allowance for another ten weeks – a total of £2 10s, at which point the police intervened.

Elizabeth White lost her own baby, but many other illegitimate 'war babies' survived, and it was not long before their plight came to the attention of seasoned campaigners like Mrs Pankhurst, who took her support for the war effort still further by taking an interest in this growing social and moral crisis. Undeterred by the disapproval of her colleagues in the suffrage campaign, she acquired four such babies and in 1916, established them in a home at 50 Clarendon Road, Kensington, London with a nurse to care for them.

The following year, the remaining funds of the Women's Social and Political Union, her suffrage organisation, were used to purchase a four-storey residence called Tower Cressy in Kensington, which was intended to be a home for female orphans. In 1919, the project was transferred to the care of trustees and was named the War Memorial Adoption Home, the now famous flagship building of the National Children's Adoption Association (NCAA) which had been set up in 1917 primarily to deal with the adoption of war babies.

Meanwhile, in Duxhurst Village, Reigate, the Babies' Haven was receiving illegitimate babies to be cared for so that their mothers could go out and rebuild their lives. It was the project of Lady Henry Somerset, a famous temperance campaigner and social activist, who now turned her considerable energies to the plight of the nation's young. In an appeal for support for the haven, she wrote of the high infant mortality in the country:

> *The reasons for this high death rate are many, among them the general disorganisation of home life, the employment of women in munitions and war work, and the entire absence of foster mothers, who are engaged in remunerative labour of all kinds. The unmarried mother has now nowhere to place her baby in safety. The baby is either hopelessly neglected and dies, or she must, in order to support it, give up her work, and perhaps drift into a life of wrong-doing to get the money to maintain herself and the child – thus bringing about still greater disaster ... Babies are a national asset; in the years before the war eight and a half million more babies were born in Germany than in England, and the mortality among children was much lower ... every child in the land must be saved.*

Of the Haven, Lady Somerset says, 'The unmarried mothers have their share of responsibility, and not only pay 5s a week, but have to furnish the name of a guarantor, who in the case of no payment, is responsible for the money.' Hopefully, these babies were the lucky ones who never fell into the hands of a wartime baby farmer.

Another imaginative if rather utopian solution was put forward by a columnist in the *British Journal of Nursing* in March 1916. In an article entitled 'Babies' Camps', the author attempts to address not only the evils of baby farming or inadequate foster care for single mothers, but also the shortage of labour on the nation's farms which was affecting the nation's wartime food supply. The author sets the scene:

> *They* [illegitimate babies] *are born for the most part in maternity homes, lying-in hospitals or in workhouse infirmaries. It is only in the last institution that the mother can, if she so wishes, remain in touch with her infant ... this course, if beneficial to the child, is disastrous to the young mother, as her surroundings tend to her demoralisation. At the end of a month the girl usually returns to* [domestic] *service, or other work, and places her infant with strangers at a payment of 5s a week with milk at 5d a quart.*

The author then goes on to describe the all too familiar tale of neglect that caused minded-out babies to fail to thrive, due to ignorance and by penny pinching – some babies were given one part milk to five parts of barley water, to make the foster fees go further, and this despite the fact that the Infant Life Protection Act had ensured the registration of minders.

The other option, we are told, is Babies' Homes but where large numbers of babies are kept together, the mortality rate was very high, understandably so with little protection against childhood diseases such as measles and whooping cough. Furthermore, 'Boy babies are the more difficult to rear, and ... the coming generation will have to make good the waste of manhood in this deplorable war.'

Turning her attention to the countryside, the author goes on to explain the serious lack of labour in the farming industry:

> *it is impossible to get the milking done ... crops are spoiled with weeds, and the sowing cannot be accomplished. Then there are the bee industries, and market and nursery gardening ... when*

so much is said about the economy of making every foot of land
produce, acres are lying idle, and hundreds of strong young girls
are ... in dull occupations, and their infants are pining and dying
amongst strangers.

The author exhorts the public to put aside any prejudices they may have
about unmarried mothers and give them a chance to redeem themselves
by their going to live in 'Baby Camps' for baby's first year. In these
places, 'the eternal laundry that seems to be at present the one and only
suitable occupation for the institutional unmarried mother, could well be
carried on in the vicinity of the camp', but the mothers could also work
on the land as much needed agricultural labour. Now the author gets
positively poetic:

The picture arises up before us of little brown [suntanned, i.e.,
healthy] *infants lying about on sweet-smelling heather or daisy-*
dappled meadows. We can see ... the sheds, each with its little
cot besides the mother's bed ... we can figure out amongst them
our very best babies' nurse, who must have a laughing face and
rosy cheeks, and who must love the babies. It is the dinner hour
and back come the mothers with flying feet to snatch up her ...
little possession and kiss and cuddle it.

All that was needed now that this vision had been put forward, enthuses
the author, is a rich benefactor to make the project happen – needless to
say, in a time of war, none came forward – but it is another example of
the body of opinion that mothers and their babies should be kept together,
to the benefit of both parties.

The NSPCC had continued its activities during the war, utilising
female inspectors for the first time as many of their male counterparts
had joined the armed forces. They also joined the widespread campaign
to promote the well-being of mothers and babies (legitimate or otherwise)
– in 1917, Robert Parr, the Director of the NSPCC, stated in a speech that
after the question of how to win the war, the issue of child welfare was of
utmost importance to the nation. He put forward two strong propositions:
first, that a child has a right to be properly born (that is, safely and in
hygienic conditions); and secondly, that the child has a right to proper
treatment after it is born.

"OUR INNOCENCE IS ALL A SHAM"

These ideas may sound obvious to the modern reader, but to some at this time, the idea that any child could have 'rights' must have been a challenge. Although Mr Parr urged all parties – voluntary, local authorities and private individuals – to work together for the sake of the nation's children to overcome adverse conditions and the ill-effects of 'habit', he also said that the ideal method was to properly prepare the parent for the fulfilment of parental duties rather than take over from them; however, if the child's rights to proper care were not being fulfilled by the parents, then the state should secure their enforcement.

Many of the voluntary bodies referred to by Mr Parr were enthusiastically taking the initiative at this time and promoting good parenting and especially (as it was popularly known) mothercraft. At the National Baby Week Exhibition in July 1917, the National Clean Milk Society had a display showing the correct and incorrect ways to keep milk in the home, and the Jewish Maternity and Sick Room Helps Society had a display of items – cot, basket, and clothes for baby – made in a pre-natal class. The *British Journal of Nursing*, who reported on the event, added, 'The importance of pre natal work is slowly receiving recognition.'

Nineteen-seventeen was also the year that National Baby Week began, heralding the era of orderly and 'scientific' child rearing where routine, cleanliness and discipline is the norm. As the interwar period continued, the pressure on parents to be 'perfect' intensified, and for adoptive parents, they had to be even better than the rest. The following year, the Maternity and Child Health Act was passed, which gave local authorities the powers to set up day nurseries and child welfare clinics, and to employ health visitors.

This Act was a consolidation of the 1907 Notification of Births Act, which decreed that the local Medical Officer of Health must be informed as soon as possible after a baby was born, and a trained health visitor would then call on the mother and advise her on how best to look after her baby. The establishment's dismay over the poor condition of the working-class men who joined the army had galvanised them into doing something about the nation's human resources, and in future, the health of babies and children was inextricably tied up with preoccupations over the health of the nation as a whole. As another writer in the *British Journal of Nursing* put it in 1917:

83

If ... National Baby Week is to make any permanent difference to the health of the nation its effect must be very far reaching ... Those into whose hands the task of teaching and uplifting the parents of the race is given must be men and women of education ... it is not enough to have a committee of gentlewomen with heaps of sympathy and little knowledge of the practical side ... The war found us unprepared to meet our enemy abroad; do let us bend all our energies towards preparation for the fight before us at home ... [the mothercraft instructors] *have to set a high standard of refinement both morally and physically and help their sisters live up to it.*

The Salvation Army was still involved in adoption at this time, striving to find new homes for very young children who had been left orphans by the war. As always, these were recorded in the Army's adoption books, sometimes with tantalising extra snippets of information such as who had the baby's ration book and what the occupation of the adoptive father was.

There was a small rise in the instances of baby farming during the war – due to the rising number of illegitimate babies being born – and correspondingly, there was also a decline in the number of respectable foster parents, many former foster mothers now being occupied in jobs for the war effort.

It may also be that the greater supervision and regulation of foster homes following the 1908 Children Act deterred those who could not meet the required standards – but sadly, not all. In November 1918, Martha Malster, a widow in Manor Park, London, received a sentence of two months' imprisonment with hard labour (the law allowed for up to six months) for undertaking the maintenance of a baby for reward and failing to notify the West Ham Guardians of this. Malster had previously had a foster child removed from her house because it was deemed unfit for the purpose of childcare, and she was told that she must not take on another child without the permission of the guardians. However, she did just that, taking a payment of £15 to foster a child for a couple, which was regarded as trafficking in the adoption of children.

As the war came to an end, Prime Minister David Lloyd George made a speech declaring that the demobbed servicemen should come home to a land fit for heroes, marking the beginning of a campaign to replace inferior housing for labouring people with quality rented accommodation. Added to the growing demand for legalised adoption and greater regulation of the welfare of children, it seemed that the post war era promised greater material comfort and more stable families. The reality was to be a rather more mixed picture.

CHAPTER 3

The Push for Legal Adoption 1918–1926

The Aftermath of World War One

By 1920, the number of live births outside marriage registered in England and Wales was 44,947, a significant increase from the figure of 37,329 in 1914. This naturally led to an increase in the number of babies in need of a new home.

These statistics did not include babies born within a marriage but not the biological child of the husband. Add to this the number of war orphans, and the devastating effect of the Spanish Influenza epidemic (which caused more than a quarter of a million deaths in Britain alone), and a serious 'surplus' of babies needing families was emerging.

Even more worrying was the fact that the infant mortality rate of illegitimate children was double that of those born within a marriage, a clear indication that welfare issues also needed to be urgently addressed. The top-left postcard on Plate 5 shows that it was not just women who were left with children to care for – the influenza epidemic took the lives of many wives and mothers and there were fathers who had to put their children in institutions because they could not cope.

Pressure to do something about the latest crisis in illegitimate births and the mothers of these babies continued to grow. On Valentine's Day 1918 the National Council for the Unmarried Mother and her Child (NCUMC) was founded in response to these pressures. Unusually, the NCUMC had no denominational or political affiliations and campaigned vigorously for a more sympathetic approach to the plight of the unmarried mother and her child. Initially, it offered support, advice and help with finding accommodation and work, but it did not assist with adoption placements – it had a policy of attempting to keep mother and baby together on the grounds that if a first-time single mother kept her child and looked after it herself, the renewed self-respect would prevent her from 'falling' again.

THE PUSH FOR LEGAL ADOPTION

The NCUMC was founded at the National Conference organised by the Child Welfare Council of the Social Welfare Association for London, a conference that was the result of a Child Welfare Inquiry, established by the Social Welfare Association in 1914. However, by the early 1920s both the NCAA and the NCUMC were both pressing for legalised adoption, if only for the pragmatic reason that adoption was happening anyway, so it needed to be regulated and better protection created for the children involved in the process.

There were not only adoption societies and dedicated mother and baby organisations working in this area, however; there were general moral welfare groups too. The Hull Vigilance Association had avowed aims of helping girls they regarded as being in moral danger because of their lifestyle, unhealthy influences or threat of abuse. They would visit music halls and theatres to 'remove' inappropriate dress, song sheets and script, and also, this being a port, boarded ships to 'rescue' any girls on board – in 1919/20 they assisted nearly 900 girls found on ships as part of their endeavours to reduce the trafficking of women.

Unmarried mothers were an equally large part of their work. In 1919, the association had dealt with 165 affiliation cases and out of 120 summons issued, 115 were successful, the remaining being rejected for lack of corroborative evidence. It took the matter of the unmarried mother and her child very seriously indeed and strove to help them stay together – a speaker at their annual conference on 5 October 1920 declared that when it came to maternity services, the single mother must be treated the same as any married mother and given access to all the same services and activities alongside everyone else, not excluded and segregated. They believed that mother and illegitimate baby must be kept together, and 'the method of "adoption" only employed in peculiar circumstances'.

They supported parents who sought advice over 'at risk' daughters, found situations for girls who needed them, and also secured four nursing girls, presumably so that the birth mother could go back to work again. They gave clothing to girls and their babies and had a staff of 'lady visitors' who paid visits to over 2,000 homes and who had contact with various other branches for mutual support.

Refreshingly, the speaker – Mrs A.C. Gotto, OBE, who was also the secretary of the National Council for Combating Venereal Diseases – also suggested that there would be fewer unwanted pregnancies among single women in the future if children had access to decent teaching about the

87

facts of life, 'so as not to allow them to face life in the ignorance that they of this generation faced it'. One wonders what the reaction of her audience would have been when she explained that by education she meant 'all decent measures which would induce decent knowledge of sex, and an appreciation of the cleanliness and beauty of sex'. Mrs Gotto also advocated a greater involvement by the father and generally an improvement in the position and protection of the single mother and her baby, 'once the child became inevitable'.

However, prejudice still continued against women who had made the same mistake more than once. A year after the Hull conference, a heated debate was going on in Devon over the unmarried mothers in the care of the Newton Abbot Board of Guardians, as they were being allowed to leave their baby at the institution so they could work. One body of opinion declared that one could not impose what looked like a custodial sentence on an unmarried mother who, having made one mistake, was expected to stay with the child until it was old enough to face the world. The opposing view was that the Guardians were being taken for a ride and unscrupulous mothers were 'dumping' their children on the authorities.

A Dr Ley took a more pragmatic view. He could see nothing wrong with allowing the unmarried mother to go out to work, but where the mother of several illegitimate children who had brought them to the institution 'had become incorrigible or so weakened in her intellectual power that she was no longer able to restrain herself, she could not be allowed to continually go out ... Every help should be given to a girl who has made a mistake ... If we are all punished for our single mistakes it will be very hard lines.' Once again, the most sympathetic treatment went to the girl who had erred the once and had the better chance of 'redemption'.

Another consequence of the war was a soaring divorce rate. In 1914 there were 856 divorces in England and Wales; by 1921, shortly after the majority of servicemen had been demobbed and gone home, it had risen to an all-time high of 3,522. This may look miniscule by modern standards, but it was enough in those maritally conservative days to chill the hearts of those who held marriage to be a sacrosanct lifelong commitment. It also meant that a larger number of children could be in single parent households with a more uncertain income coming in, making them vulnerable to an unsettled future, but adoption societies tended to be reluctant to accept the children of divorced couples onto their lists.

Back to the Home

By the 1920s, a new set of pressures and influences was starting to shape people's views of the family and their role in it – especially for women. Many families now had far fewer children than the previous generations and women who had gladly taken over the roles of the men who were on the Front Line were now being exhorted to be the perfect stay-at-home wife and mother.

A proliferation of women's magazines such as *Lady's Companion* and *Home Chat* enthusiastically endorsed the idea that being at home was the perfect way to live, calling its reader 'Little Wife' and featuring fictional stories about young married women who made the terrible mistake of thinking they could have a career and a family, and who paid a price for their audacity. *Home Chat* featured smiling, immaculate housewives in crisp aprons on its cover, alongside subheadings about short stories and featured sewing patterns.

An evening at the cinema could leave a young woman wishing that she too could have that comfortable home in the suburbs and mature into a respectable married matron and pillar of the community and of the local Women's Institute – because the girls in films who were 'no better than they ought to be' almost always ended the story alone, friendless and in disgrace. It was a world which middle-class women could aspire to, and working-class women would dream about – but always it included the perfect small family of two or three well-mannered, intelligent and good-looking children.

In this highly ordered home, with its aromas of freshly baked cakes and crisp new curtains, children were to be raised in a rigid routine, and many women were cajoled by the child rearing 'experts', such as Sir Frederic Truby King, to stick to certain practices regardless of the personality or needs of the individual child. In the Truby King home nursery, babies were fed strictly to a four hour routine during the day, put in their own room from birth and put out in their prams for hours in the fresh air to toughen them up. Cuddles were limited to a matter of minutes each day. One can imagine the conflict some mothers faced in trying to adhere to a routine which often went against their every instinct. One can also easily imagine that many adopted children would be deeply unsettled by it, after the disrupted start to life they may have experienced, and later in life may have wondered if they were victims of a drive for perfection.

Even if women did not use these draconian methods of child rearing, many subtle pressures were placed on her to raise her baby in a certain way. Plate 7 shows a typical magazine advertisement aimed at the new mother. Featured in *Punch* magazine, 23 April 1924, it perfectly illustrates these new pressures – the close attention of the professionals, nurses and doctors on mother and baby; the use of artificial feeding as an aid to maintaining strict routines; and an overall ambience of order and cleanliness. It was not enough for a married woman to aspire to an ideal of housewifery – now, she must also be a certain type of mother as well. Adopted mothers especially were expected to be paragons of motherhood.

However, it was not just a drive for perfection; it was also a way of 'rescuing' innocent children from the sorry background in which they started out. No longer would these 'at risk' children and babies face the prospect of growing up in the care of a woman who had dubious morals and lacked self-control; instead, they would be well nourished, soundly educated and morally guided by their new parents, and live in a nice house with every facility where respectability and cleanliness were the watchwords. In a sense, it was a 'cure' for the ills visited on the child by its unfortunate mother. This was the ideal that was propagandised by some, although it was not always achieved, and in one way it gave birth mothers no more empathy or regard than the Victorians had done 40 years earlier.

These were also the decades when family size limitation began to have an impact. According to the Royal Commission on Population which researched the subject as part of its remit in 1946, more than half of the married women questioned who had married in the first half of the 1920s, used some form of contraception to regulate their fertility, and those who married at the beginning of the 1930s and used contraception were by far in the majority. This was in stark contrast to their mother's generation – of those women questioned who married at the beginning of the twentieth century, five out of six of them did not regulate their families at all.

The most famous proponent of family limitation, Marie Stopes, wrote her famous book, *Married Love*, on the subject in 1918. In 1921, she opened her first family planning clinic in London, then moved it to the city centre in 1925; by 1930, a whole network of other organisations sprang up to fulfil the interest in their services, and they all joined together to form the National Birth Control Council (later called the

Family Planning Association). A glib description of the facts cannot describe the outrage that was caused by this development from moral campaigners and various religious denominations, but such was the demand, from married women especially, that this new trend was unstoppable.

George, Duke of York and his pretty wife Elizabeth, who became King George VI and Queen Elizabeth in 1936, epitomised this perfect small family, with their daughters Elizabeth ('Lilibet') and Margaret Rose filling many a magazine feature with relaxed photographs. They were widely revered by the public as the ultimate in small family respectability. Plate 6 shows the Duke and Duchess on the eve of the Duke's coronation as King George VI, the proud parents of two beautifully turned out little girls – the Duke is even wearing a lounge suit and the Duchess is wearing a simple afternoon dress and jewellery; they are also a wonderful example of how the family had shrunk since the days of the Duke's grandmother, Queen Victoria, who was equally revered in her day for her large brood of nine children and rapidly expanding extended family.

During the interwar period the small family of a few much loved and cherished children became the norm, as opposed to the large numbers of children in families of the previous century. Their lives somehow seemed less valuable because there were so many of them, and because parents expected some of them to die before they reached adulthood. Fewer children meant a greater investment in those that were born.

Imagine then the pressure on a young married couple who were expected to produce their first offspring within a couple of years of marriage; it was common practice to carefully put away the bottom tier of a wedding cake (with the added preservative of an extra splash of rum or brandy) in a tin, to be used as the christening cake when baby came along, but if baby did not put in an appearance, what would people say? It almost became one of the 'rituals of respectability' to have a baby to complete the new family and grace the nursery, perhaps as an affirmation that this was a real family unit and worthy of respect.

As time went by, for a couple who were not able to conceive, or who were struggling with repeated miscarriages or stillbirths, the questions and hints about their tardiness in producing a child would become at best tiresome, and at worst deeply upsetting, a constant reminder of their failure to be that ideal family unit. There was a widely held belief that childless couples were 'selfish' or cold-hearted, in a sense, not 'playing the game'. In an era when conformity was the safest path to tread, anyone who could not conform was threatened with disapproval.

If the compulsion or pressure to have a baby to complete the family always dreamed of became overwhelming, options for married couples were limited. Fertility treatments were very much in their early stages – attempts to treat blocked fallopian tubes only began in the 1920s in the United States and it is likely that the majority of couples would not entertain the idea of donor sperm, however that sperm was 'delivered' to the woman.

Yet the agony of not being able to have a baby for the woman, and the humiliation for her husband of not having a complete family to take care of and provide for, meant something had to be done. There was still, for some women, the option of 'borrowing' or being given a child by a sister or mother, where families were unmanageably large – but fewer families in this period were so large that they had 'surplus' children to give away to childless relatives. This arrangement would provide a child with a genetic link to the couple, and might even afford the comfort of feeling that their child might look like them, but it would be fraught with worry – what if their relationship with the biological relative broke down and they demanded their child back? It was in many ways a situation that was literally too close to home. The only other solution was to take on the child of a stranger.

Adopting a perfect baby was seen by some as a 'solution' to their childlessness, and it was no doubt seen as a wonderful solution all round – the childless could become parents and fulfil their cultural destiny, even more secure for knowing that having passed a screening process they must be 'better' than many couples with natural children who could reproduce at will regardless of their potential to be good parents. A displaced baby gets her or his own doting parents and has the opportunity to leave behind the failure that was the birth family and be moulded into a much better class of person than they might have been. The birth mother, suitably chastened (it was hoped), could move on and rebuild her life, go to work, or get married and start afresh. And society relieves itself of a problem and a burden in the form of the single mother and her baby, having sculpted yet another perfect family unit in the process.

While all this pressure was building for people to become the perfect family, campaigners had continued to work for legislation to formalise adoption in England and Wales. In 1920, the Associated Societies for the Care and Maintenance of Infants produced a report prompted by their

1919 conference, which explored the topic of adoption. While it was agreed that the adoption of a child was so serious a step that it must be regulated by law and officially recorded, it also stated that wherever possible, the birth mother and child should be kept together. Dismissing the suggestion that adoption could reduce the number of illegitimate children being born, it also said that 'very many of these (illegitimate) children are unsuitable for adoption' anyway.

The organisation was also in favour of the many private adoption agencies springing up being subjected to official registration and some form of public control. The remark about illegitimate children is baffling and is a sad reflection of what many people still felt at that time – that these children were inferior in many ways to children who for other reasons, such as bereavement, had to leave their wholly legitimate place in their birth family.

The campaign for legal adoption was also supported by the National Council of Women, who lobbied the Home Secretary, Reginald Mckenna, on the matter. Represented by several officials, the deputation made the point that 'promiscuous adoption' was now taking place – fuelled no doubt by the higher numbers of illegitimate babies available – and indeed, adoption was becoming quite the fashionable thing to do. Mrs Edwin Gray lamented the lack of suitable foster mothers, and pointed out that unscrupulous lawyers were selling adoption 'deeds' to adoptive parents for a guinea (approximately £105 today), which, of course, had no real legal weight.

Worries were also raised about the use of the concept of adoption to disguise baby farming (which had had something of a revival due to the wartime 'baby boom') and of the habit of taking on a child simply to have it work for the family when old enough. Mr McKenna responded favourably to the deputation, saying the matter was not contentious, and also added rather ambiguously that many people looked upon children as a legitimate investment for their old age. Yet, he did promise to look into appointing a committee to investigate the matter.

Adoption Societies

In the meantime, many adoption societies had sprung up to fulfil the demand for potential parents to adopt children and babies. At the annual meeting of the National Children's Adoption Association (NCAA) in 1925, it was announced that the number of children adopted between 1

June 1919 and 31 March 1925 was 1,153, of whom 556 had passed through the famous hostel at Tower Cressy, the imposing building in Kensington.

Because of the upmarket building, genteel ambience and well connected supporters, reports of the venture were benevolent in their descriptions of the facilities. In 1920, the *British Journal of Nursing* (Midwife Supplement) wrote of the balconies ideal for children to sleep or play on, the impressive views from the upper floors and the roof, and the nursery with its treasure cots with white coverlets with embroidery on them. At the top of the building where there would be little through foot traffic, was the isolation ward. Also at the top of the building was the flat occupied by Miss Clara Andrew, the founder and Honorary Director, whose project it had been since its earlier incarnation as the Children Adoption Association in 1918.

Each child had her or his own washing requisites, carefully labelled, and there was a special room for the preparation of feeding bottles. The description emphasises the cheerful and loving atmosphere of the place, and the dedication of the Matron, Miss Florence Borrett, but then somewhat spoils the effect by reflecting,

Sad that such a work as this Home stands for should be needed, but no one who has been in touch with the seamy side of life can doubt its necessity and humanity ... before receiving children for adoption, they must be medically examined and their history gone into and furnished to the prospective adopters. First children only are received. All honour to this who have stretched out a helping and discerning hand to a most pitiable section of society.

As this was written in 1920, it is perhaps not surprising that the Victorian caveats of the 'once fallen woman', healthy child and scrutiny of birth family background are being undertaken, with a long way to go before the birth family themselves are given any consideration in the whole process. Another factor in common with many child-centred organisations was a desire to acquire well known patrons – the President was Princess Alice, and one of the Vice Presidents was Mrs Stanley Baldwin; later on, the eminent John Galsworthy was a prominent supporter who championed their campaign for funds to repair the building.

It is because of its prominent support, its prestigious building at a 'good' address and its well publicised 'high' standards, by 1925, 556 children had passed through Tower Cressy and were adopted, out of a total of 1,153 children adopted between 1919 and March 1925. One cannot help thinking this is an unrealistically low number of total adoptions in England and Wales, based only on statistics from adoption agencies and societies, and not including the many informal inter-family and third party adoptions which occurred without generating any arrangement more formal than a handshake, if that. By the end of 1926, NCAA advertisements proudly stated that 'A Child is Adopted Every Day' via their organisation.

In the continued absence of a legal form of adoption, less salubrious adoptions continued to take place, babies were still bought and sold, and adoptive parents still broke the law in an attempt to make a child appear to be their natural child for whatever reason. In 1921, it was revealed in court that a Mrs Holden paid the huge amount of £200 (the equivalent of £21,228 today) to Elinor Mary Cooper for her to adopt her baby girl and register her as her own biological child. Cooper tried to register the child as her own, even giving her her own name, but they were found out and instead of heading off to Africa with her husband to start a new life, the mother and Cooper found themselves in court. Needless to say, the child had died and an inquest was held, but as the reason for the child's death was blood poisoning; it could not be directly attributed to any cause such as neglect.

The NSPCC supported legal adoption, but only if satisfactory safeguards for the children to be adopted were built into the law. Between 1922 and 1923, the society had dealt with 32,239 cases of neglect, and presumably felt they had good reason to fear that an inadequate adoption law could place children in inferior homes which would lead to yet more such cases.

The 1926 Adoption of Children Act
As a result of the growing support among adoption societies, politicians and other agencies concerned with child welfare, several attempts were made to guide adoption bills through Parliament in the early 1920s. The Hopkinson Committee set up in 1920 concluded that legal adoption would be a positive step forward, and the Tomlin Committee of 1924 also endorsed the perceived positive effects legalised adoption would have, however, it raised questions over some issues, for instance over the merits

of breaking all ties with the birth family, although in effect the subsequent act set the precedent for the cutting of all ties and only rarely did the birth family maintain a link with their now adopted child after 1926.

By the mid-1920s, a bill had been introduced to Parliament to legalise and regulate the adoption of children. It was the tenth bill to be introduced on this subject since 1922. Based on the recommendations of the Tomlin Committee, it still must have been extremely challenging for those who had to draft the bill to be mindful of the many points of view and agendas of those involved, and the Committee interviewed dozens of witnesses in its attempts to take a broad view.

Although in general the bill was favourably received in Parliament, both as a pragmatic way of improving the lives of many children, and as a patriotic way of mending some of the problems caused by the Great War, the bill was not welcomed by all members of parliament. Lieutenant Commander Kenworthy, the Labour MP for Hull Central, declared in a debate on 3 April 1925, that such a bill would 'encourage the breaking up of families and the shirking of the duties of parenthood' and he believed that it was part of a trend towards the breakdown of family if birth parents, for reasons of poverty, lack of feeling for a child, or sheer selfishness used the courts to transfer their legal parenthood to adoptive parents.

He went on to say that the bill would also enable parents who had been too selfish to have children themselves and who later in life had a gap in their lives, to go to poor people with large families and induce them to part with one of their children. In opposition to this view were many people who simply wanted to safeguard the new families created by an adoption, by putting it in a legal framework and formally transferring parental rights.

Finally, the long awaited and debated act to legalise adoption became law on 1 January 1927. No one seems to have thought it perfect – in fact, on 11 May 1925 *The Times* declared the report on which the bill was based to be 'cautious and limited' in character. Rather it was seen as a good starting point, and indeed it did cover most of the important points that had been agonised over and it provided important reassurances for adoptive parents, not least the peace of mind that came with knowing that the fear of birth parents materialising and demanding their child back had been lifted. It also gave confidentiality – only in the newly established Adopted Children Register could the original birth record be traced.

CHILD DESERTION IN WORCESTERSHIRE.

The abandoned baby: abandonment or desertion was one of the unpalatable options available to the desperate single mother (*The Pictorial Times*, 1846). (Author's collection)

Later in the nineteenth century, the cause of the 'fallen woman' was taken up with enthusiasm by various social action movements and faith based organisations. Illustration circa 1900. (Author's collection)

(*Above*) Queen Victoria's large brood of children made the big patriarchal family seem eminently respectable and desirable. (*Illustrated London News*, 12 July 1856). (*Below*) Large Institutions such as this orphanage near Croydon looked impressive to the outside world, but did not present as a home from home to the children inside them. (Author's collection)

THE REEDHAM ORPHANAGE.

THE IRONING-ROOM.

(*Above*) Children in orphanages were taught practical skills to enable them to support themselves after they left the institution. (*Below*) An alternative and smaller scale form of accommodation for the child without a family: the Dr Barnardo's Village Homes for Girls, Barkingside. (Author's collection)

Dr. BARNARDO'S HOMES.

A VIEW OF THE GIRLS' VILLAGE HOMES, BARKINGSIDE.

(*Above left*) By 1919-1920, many orphans had been created by the ravages of World War I, and the Spanish Flu epidemic. It was not always children who had lost mothers who were given up for adoption; lone fathers had to do it too. (*Above right*) 'Playing the Field'. The 1939-45 war replicated the atmosphere of "live for today" that had been generated in the First World War, leading to an upsurge in illegitimate births. (Author's collection)

(*Above*) Many children's charities were adept at fundraising, using a variety of activities to pay for much needed resources. (*Right*) Adoption societies were reluctant to advertise in a blatant way, but found fundraising advertisements an effective method of raising their profile and 'name dropping' important benefactors. (Author's collection)

(*Above*) The equivalent of media celebrities of today, the Duke and Duchess of York and their daughters epitomised the ideal of the small modern family of the 1920s and 1930s. From an informal photograph, 1937. (*Below*) Images of happy, well adjusted children were the ideal advertisement for any adoption society – useful for encouraging goodwill and donations. (Church of England Children's Society (formerly Waifs and Strays) postcard, used as a thank you note in response to a donation.) (Author's collection)

CHURCH OF ENGLAND CHILDREN'S SOCIETY
(Formerly "Waifs and Strays")
OLD TOWN HALL, KENNINGTON ROAD, LONDON, S.E.11
Secretary: Colonel E. St. J. Birnie

T H A N K

Y O U

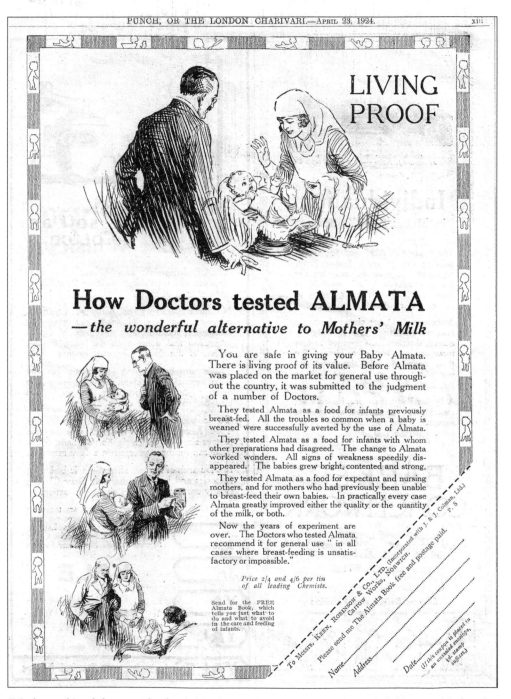

'Mothercraft' and the growth of a field of expert knowledge of baby and child care added to the pressures on women to create the perfect family. Advertisement from *Punch* magazine, 23 April 1924, for Almata, an artificial baby milk. (Author's collection)

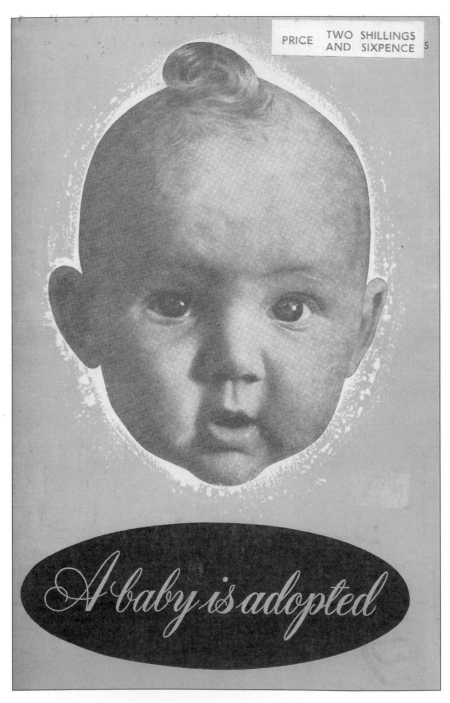

PRICE TWO SHILLINGS AND SIXPENCE s

A baby is adopted

By the post 1945 era, the adoption 'industry' was well populated with experts who would advise and guide would-be parents through the adoption process. (Cover of the booklet, *A Baby is Adopted: The Children's Society's Adoption Book,* by Margaret Kornitzer, published by The Church of England Children's Society, London, 1950.) (Author's collection)

However, it did not guarantee strict secrecy. Age restrictions were put in place; the adoptive parents had to be at least 25 years of age and they also had to be more than 21 years older than the child to be adopted, while the child to be adopted had to be under the age of 21 years. No sole male adoptive parent would be allowed to adopt a female child except in exceptional circumstances, an obvious attempt to forestall any potentially abusive situations.

Furthermore, the adoption order could not be issued unless all those who had an interest in the child, be they parents, guardians, those with responsibility for the custody of the child, etc., had given full agreement, again, a safeguard for adoptive parents so that no one could return to the issue later and claim they had not agreed and demand the return of the child. Also, where a married couple were to be the child's new parents, both spouses had to give consent for the adoption to go ahead. Adoptive parents had to be resident in England and Wales, to prevent any trafficking of children onto the continent or elsewhere, and to try to prevent financial gain when it came to adoptions, no person wishing to adopt could receive or agree to receive any money in respect of the adoption except in rare cases where a court had sanctioned it (a clear reference to the ghastly practice of baby farming which still survived albeit to a much lesser degree than before).

Any court making an adoption order also had to make sure that the birth parent/s clearly understood the implications of what they were doing; in short, signing away all legal rights, forever, to act as parent to the child concerned. Emphasis is also given to the notion that the adoption order must be made in the best interests of the child and no one else. The specific circumstances of the illegitimate child born to unmarried parents who later married was dealt within a separate act.

There is a sense of finality in the wording of the Adoption of Children Act – it tries to protect the adoptive parents (and from the child's point of view, their new parents and stable home life) from any future disruption or upset from the child's 'past life'. Emphasis was placed on a 'fresh start' and birth parents or family had been largely excluded, and every attempt made to give the newly constructed family the privacy and security to move forward without shadows from the past looming over them. The child had a new name that was enshrined in law, with a new birth certificate in the adoptive family's surname. First names were easily changed too, especially with a baby who as yet had no understanding of what a name was and could not answer to it. The shutters were brought down on an old life and family, and the only one that mattered henceforward was the new one.

The Act was in some ways not as radical as certain lobby groups would have wanted, however. Perhaps as a result of the comments in the Committee report by Mr Justice Tomlin, baby farming was not touched upon. The Government took the view that the bill was not designed to do away with baby farming, which would be better dealt with by an amendment to the 1908 Children Act, according to Mr Locker-Hampson of the Home Office. It also left a curious loophole whereby an adopted child could still, in cases of intestacy, inherit from birth parents, which is curious because ties with the birth family were supposed to be at an end after the adoption, but this would be addressed in subsequent legislation.

In addition, the Government took a rather disapproving view of the relatively large-scale adoptions arranged by adoption societies, declaring them to 'have given to adoption a prominence which is somewhat artificial and may not be in all respects wholesome', to an extent reflecting the views of the MP for Hull Central above. It was also suggested that the relationship to be created – that of adoptive child and parents – was entirely contrived and really had no 'naturalness' about it at all. *The Times* put it much more starkly: 'It is an artificial doctrine, wholly alien to our social traditions' (11 May 1925).

With hindsight, that seems an insult to the passionate devotion and commitment many adoptive parents invested in their new offspring, but the comment was almost swimming against a tide – the tide of the brave new world of the legally constructed family. The establishment's shock at the poor state of the labouring poor had started to have an impact, and no longer could families be allowed completely free rein to have children as and when they wanted, and to keep them under any circumstances. State intervention was at last part of family life, and this involvement was to intensify over the next 25 years, not decrease. The legislation was, as Sir Alfred Hopkinson said in 1925, 'a step in a forward movement for the protection of children.'

Although private adoptions were to continue for some time to come, for various reasons, the legal route provided by the 1926 Act was immediately popular with many ordinary adoptive parents and birth parents who wished to have a certain future for their children. In the first year of its operation, 3,173 adoption orders were issued, and two-thirds of all the minors adopted were illegitimate; 85 per cent of the adoptive parents were married couples adopting jointly. Some illegitimate children were also given security in another way, by the Legitimacy Act of 1926 – where a couple were living together and had children but were not married, if the children were from that couple, if the couple subsequently married the children were automatically deemed to be legitimate.

'Not in Front of the Children': Adoption and Secrecy

What Acts of Parliament fail to do, however, is eradicate from people's minds and hearts the images and feelings of the past. It was considered a good thing for the birth mother to be able to make a clean break from the baby, thus allowing her the chance to start again and leave her indiscretion, humiliation and heartache behind. The relative secrecy of legal adoption meant as few people as possible need know of her mistake and she would be able to move forward without the temptation of thinking she would like her baby back.

Of course, in practice, most birth mothers suffered years of grieving following the adoption of their baby. Adopted children still often grew up knowing or even just 'feeling' that they were 'different' to their family, often not able to identify what that difference could be; it did nothing to appease an adoptive parent's anxieties about a child who grew up to be unlike them in looks, habits and opinions (often wrongly attributed to the child's 'bad start in life'). The Act also may well have deterred some people from coming forward to legally adopt, as they felt they would not be eligible or feared the scrutiny of officials.

As a result, and possibly also because of the innate suspicion human beings have of new developments, private adoptions continued alongside the newly legal ones. Secrecy was important to many couples, as there was undoubtedly a fear of the stigma of infertility, which the revelation of having to adopt a child might imply, and even worse, one day they might have to reveal to the child that she or he was illegitimate.

This led to an unfortunate correlation between adoption and failure and did nothing to encourage some people to follow the legal route to adopting a child. Sometimes it was kept secret for better reasons – a child who was known to be adopted at school would be assumed to be illegitimate and could be bullied as a result. In fact, anything that raised the spectre of the birth family was feared by many adoptive parents. If a child grew up knowing she or he was adopted, they might want contact with birth family, or even worse, if the birth family knew where the child was, they might suddenly turn up and demand contact or even blackmail the adoptive family by threatening to reveal the arrangement.

A child who knew they were adopted may grow up suffering feelings of rejection and from the adoptive parents' point of view, they sometimes feared that the child they had worked so hard to adopt may not love them in the same way as a natural child would. And what if the child asked questions about their origins which the adoptive parents could not answer, or did not want to answer because they felt the child's origins were not respectable – because they were illegitimate? All these factors threatened to undermine this carefully constructed new family in its suburban setting built on respectability and keeping oneself to oneself. If any of their business seeped out to their neighbours, it would lead to a huge loss of face.

There were many pressing reasons to keep an adoption quiet where at all possible, and the 1926 Act reinforced this point of view. The secrecy was unfortunate when one considers that some of those involved in the process would have felt the need to confide in someone about how they felt about the process. Both birth and adoptive parents could have benefited from talking things through with welfare workers or the family doctor, but this was an era when anything approaching counselling was virtually unheard of. The ethos of adoption was determinedly cheerful; all three parties were considered to have gained benefit from it, so what need would there be for therapy of any kind? Minority support groups were equally unknown and in any case, all parties involved had a vested interest in avoiding the stigma of public knowledge. For those who felt themselves to be a victim of the process, it had to be a private suffering.

There were also people who continued to use the idea of adoption as a means of financial gain. As we will see in the next chapter, in May 1932, Walter and Mary Field from Lincolnshire were charged with conspiring to obtain money by false pretences, following the insertion of adverts in local newspapers regarding child adoption – this was exactly the kind of publicity regarding adoption that campaigners hoped to avoid.

CHAPTER 4

From Perfect Families to Disrupted Lives 1926–1945

How Legal Adoption Fared

It is almost inevitable that the arrival of legal adoption took some time to embed in the national consciousness as the right way forward, and that mistakes would be made with the choice some agencies made in adoptive parents. No area of childcare is immune from stories of mistreatment, and that includes adoption.

Despite the economic slump which affected Britain in the interwar period, adoptions were relatively resilient to the recession. In September 1932, the London County Council, which was looking after 8,500 homeless children, told the press that there was a 'steady demand by good class people, many in really affluent circumstances, for the adoption of children. They are not all people without children. We often get applications from parents with a family of three or more.'

The NCAA continued to work hard to place babies with new families in the 1930s, and their proud boast at this time was that no baby spent more than 30 days at Tower Cressy, and indeed, some babies were there only a few days, such was the demand for their charges. In 1930, Miss Clara Andrew proudly declared that only 4 per cent of their babies were subsequently returned and that was usually because the adoptive family had been beset with unexpected financial problems. 'Most of the applications we receive come from married couples who have no children of their own,' she said to the press and added, 'More and more unmarried women each year are adopting children. Many of them are schoolteachers.'

The willingness of the adoption societies to accept single women as applicants is interesting. After the war, there was an estimated 239,000 surplus women between the ages of 25 and 34 according to statistics from the 1921 census, and many commentators at the time fretted over the wasted potential of these 'surplus' women who should have married and had children of their own. Some of these women chose not to marry, either because of the greater access to the professions and careers for those with the appropriate education or who were in jobs which expected women to leave if they got married or became pregnant, but that does not mean that they did not yearn to have a child of their own. Others may have been childless war widows. Their options were limited; such was the continuing stigma of illegitimacy that having their own biological child could not be considered, apart from the fact that having the time off for the birth and afterwards would disrupt their careers and decimate their income.

However, what of all the many babies and children in care who needed stable homes, not to mention the steady stream of illegitimate children being born every year, war or no war? To the adoption societies the solution was obvious – give these women the opportunity to adopt a child. Understandably, adoption societies did emphasise that the single women they preferred as adopters should be professionals, which was only to be expected bearing in mind that women's wages in the early 1930s were still only half those of men in many areas. Adoption societies may even have felt that in accepting unmarried women, they were allowing them to fulfil a traditional role and give them a useful maternal function in society. Professional or bluestocking women had been adopting 'stranger' children (children who were not related to them) in the nineteenth century; now adoption societies were actively courting them as adopters.

In 1930, two unmarried ladies – sisters, one of whom had a professional career – decided to adopt a child. They approached the Homeless Children's Aid and Adoption Society, a well-established organisation inaugurated in the 1890s and with offices in London, and happily a match was found for them in the form of a little girl. Despite occurring after the 1926 Act, it was to be an informal adoption with all the paperwork generated by the adoption society. Two letters have survived which give a fascinating insight into several aspects of the attitudes of the times. The first letter is dated 25 October 1930 and announces:

Dear Friends,
With reference to your wish to adopt a little girl, I am glad to
say we have a little one. — was born on — and I am arranging
for her to be here, – 93, Westminster Bridge Road – on Thursday
afternoon the 30ʰᵗ inst. at 3 o'clock. I shall be glad to have a line
from you by return to say we may expect you on Thursday next.
This will enable you to see the little girlie, and if she appeals to
you to take her back with you on a visit for a few weeks, and thus
you will be able to judge whether she settles down, and is the
little one you would like to adopt.

The letter is signed by E.T. Beesley, the secretary of the society.

The correspondence clearly continued and another letter from the society dated 7 November adds to the story:

I am in receipt of your letter. Little —'s mother was quite a nice
girl, and it was a very sad experience indeed for her when this
misfortune occurred. She was only a young woman, and very
much to be pitied, in fact, the Salvation Army friends who took
an interest in her and wrote to us on her behalf, spoke very
highly and warmly of her, as also did the Matron of the Home
where the girl stayed.

With regard to the father, I have no knowledge. The little one
was baptised in the Parish Church of —, I am enclosing you the
baptismal card and also, the certificate of registration.

Now, with regard to giving her your name. It will be necessary
for you to make an application to the Magistrates' Court in the
district in which you reside, and they will issue to you certain
papers, which will have to be filled in and signed, and if you will
send them to me, I will get them completed and return to you,
and I shall be happy to help you in any way I may be able.

The two ladies were then asked to sign a form and return it to the office of the adoption society.

The adoption did indeed go ahead, but on an informal basis at first, and the little girl had a very happy and contented childhood and as she grew up, she had no desire to look for her birth family. No doubt the two sisters were regarded as ideal adopters because of their stable home, professional income and as an added bonus, the adoption society united a little girl who needed a home with two single women who now had an extra purpose to their lives. The adoption was not legalised until 1942, for a couple of reasons – firstly, the little girl's mother had made enquiries regarding the return of her daughter, which came to nothing, but no doubt the incident unsettled the sisters; and secondly, at that time one sister adopted another little girl, so it made sense to have the status of both daughters placed on a formal footing.

Often the wording of such letters sounds archaic to the modern reader. Phrases such as 'little girlie' and 'little one' come across as patronising, and referring to the unwanted pregnancy as 'this misfortune' seems far too coy, but in fact would not be out of place in any publication of the day. Children's books and women's magazines also used language such as this, and it is unlikely that the secretary was trying to be anything other than kindly and approachable.

Meanwhile, at the NCAA, the nurses at Tower Cressy were students being trained for positions in families, learning to gain the children's affection and to build confidence by using patience and affection, and they were taught never to raise their voices in reproof. The founder, Miss Clara Andrew, had always supported legal adoption because she wished to see adoptive parents put in a stronger position legally. Having fully embraced the legal adoption of children after the 1926 Act, the NCAA advertised a free advice service to anyone interested in legally adopting a child, and proudly declared that the NCAA had no associations with any other adoption society – they saw themselves as a flagship organisation and superior to other adoption societies, despite coming under strong criticism at times in the interwar period.

Ironically, in the very same column in *The Times* newspaper that the NCAA advertisement appeared, so did an advert for the 'Birth Control Society and Pioneer Clinic' founded by Marie Stopes and situated in Whitfield Street, London: this was one of the agents of a national trend towards family limitation which was to lead to a sharp decline in adoptions and children available for adoption, decades later.

The National Adoption Society was also placing as many children with new families as possible, although one of their professed reasons for doing so was rather odd – the reduction of childcare costs to the community as a whole. In their annual report for 1932, the society stated they had arranged for 325 babies to be adopted, bringing their total over the lifetime of the society to 2,926 children. They hoped to increase this number, they said, because not only would more children have a stable and happy family life, but they would be less likely to 'drift' and require support from charity or the State in later years. Each adoption cost the society £10 3s 4d, which public donations helped to cover.

The Salvation Army was steadily adopting out children, and between 1930 and 1935 arranged 63 adoptions. Other organisations, such as religious denominations, also played their part – one Roman Catholic maternity home in London arranged twenty-one adoptions in the first half of the 1930s. Section 32 of the 1930 Poor Law Act gave permission to public assistance authorities to consent to the adoption of children in their care. It seemed that many of the bodies concerned with the welfare of the twentieth century's displaced children, were all working with a common purpose to make sure that their charges ended up in homes and families of their own.

Fundraising was on the whole genteel but quietly persistent – money came from a variety of sources, such as charitable donations and endowments, payments from birth mothers, birth fathers and adoptive parents, public appeals and the many events that charities are so adept at – flag days, garden parties, entertainments, and so on. As always, high-profile supporters were used to advance an image of respectability – Plate 5 shows the connection of Waifs and Strays Society with the Duke of Kent and his wife, Princess Marina, who are being used to raise its profile and encourage donations.

The Actors' Orphanage was still doing sterling work in the 1930s in looking after its charges, and in 1934 it acquired a very high-profile president – the actor and playwright Noel Coward. Even though the orphanage was the philanthropic product of the world of the theatre, Coward brought a touch of glamour to his role, implementing improvements to buildings and gardens. He was accompanied on his visits by high-profile friends such as Ivor Novello (who was to become a Vice President) and Edith Evans, and he transformed the Christmas parties with lavish spreads of treats.

One rather unusual treat received by the 70 children at the orphanage in 1934 was a ton of Robertson's preserves, donated by the head of the company, Robert Robertson. Coward took a proactive and empathetic interest in the orphans, and one of the children he mentored was Peter Collinge, a troubled 12-year-old who, with Coward's support, went on to become a noted film director and even directed Coward in the film *The Italian Job* in 1969. Noel Coward remained in office until he emigrated to Jamaica in 1956.

Astonishingly, even in the 1930s, baby farming was still being practised and birth parents were paying baby farmers to take their babies rather than face exposure by going to an adoption agency. On 10 May 1932, the first hearing was held into the case of Lincolnshire baby farmers Mary and Walter Field. The police discovered that at least five babies had been taken in by the Fields, receiving £13 for one of them from the birth mother. Of these five, one had died and the body had not been recovered. The Chief Constable of Lincoln, in one of his statements to the court, urged birth parents: 'before anyone parts with a little helpless child, they will have the humanity to make reasonable inquiries regarding the condition of the place – I will not say home – to which it is proposed the child should be sent.'

He added that the living conditions of the baby farmers were 'deplorable' and also said, 'I also hope that it will lead to stricter observance of the law relating to the adoption of children.' Walter Field was unemployed and the couple had no income of their own, other than the money from baby farming. Thankfully, action was taken via the Children and Young Person's Act of 1932, which banned would-be baby farmers from advertising anonymously for babies. On the other side of this issue, desperate birth parents or their families were still advertising for kindly people to take on unwanted babies: 'Wanted, Respectable Person to Adopt Baby Girl. – Write for particulars to Box 280, Herald Office, Tamworth.' (*Tamworth Herald*, 7 November 1931.)

The Horsbrugh Report
Despite the fact that many agencies were by now working hard to place as many children as they could with loving families, there was growing unease about the calibre of some of those individuals and organisations who were involved in adoption, both legalised and informal (which was still going on after the 1926 Act).

As a result, the Government appointed a Parliamentary Committee in January 1936 to look into the practices of adoption societies, under the chairmanship of Florence Horsbrugh, Member of Parliament for Dundee. Miss Horsbrugh steered the committee through 21 meetings and the interviewing of 65 witnesses, most of whom were representatives from the main adoption societies, other voluntary agencies, and local authorities who were also involved in adoption arrangement. The report of the committee was, in effect, a review of adoption for the first ten years after the 1926 Act and makes fascinating reading.

The Committee looked at four different ways to adopt a child: through adoption societies whose sole raison d'etre was to arrange adoptions; voluntary organisations and other groups who occasionally arranged adoptions; local authorities; and private individuals. The adoption societies they focused on were the National Adoption Society, the NCAA, the Homeless Children's Aid Society and Adoption Society; the National Children's Home (which had registered as an adoption society in 1926); the Mission of Hope in Croydon; the Lancashire and Cheshire Adoption Council; and the Waifs and Strays Society.

It was found that informal adoption was still very much practised, despite the 1926 Act and the increasing popularity of legal adoption, and it is surprising to read that some adoptions arranged by adoption societies were in fact not legalised – in one society there was an instance of only 30 per cent actually going through the courts, all the rest remained informal with all the disadvantages that entailed. This was, though, an unusually high number compared to many societies. The committee thought that some adoptive parents, once they had their longed-for child, simply did not bother to make the adoption legal either out of ignorance or sheer apathy (although for adoptive parents who received a child via an agency or society, it is hard to believe that they were not told what to do to make it a legal arrangement).

However, adoption societies being the main focus of the report, the committee looked in great detail at how they were run, what their accommodation was like, their treatment of adoptive parents and birth mother, and the procedures used to bring about the adoption, such as the selection of adoptive parents and the screening of birth mother and child. They found that although most of the hostel accommodation provided for the children in their care was adequate, not all was of a suitable standard. In fact, from one hostel, three children had to be admitted to a London hospital in an emaciated and neglected condition – sadly, one of these children died of enteritis soon after admission. In another area, the high death rates in a different hostel were causing alarm with the local Medical Officer of Health. Use of unsatisfactory foster parents for children awaiting adoption was also a cause for concern.

Most adoption societies had some form of selection procedure, but it varied from one to the other. Some societies had rigorous procedures for the matching and choosing of adoptive parents and babies, but others were sometimes lax in comparison. Insufficiently detailed medical checks were done on the child and their birth mother, which led to the occasional case of a baby being found to have contracted venereal disease from the birth mother, yet was still adopted out. Had this baby had a Wasserman test (the test used to ascertain if a person is infected with syphilis, which can be passed from mother to baby), this baby would never have been considered a suitable case for adoption.

The social background of the birth parents was also checked by some, and not others. Would-be adoptive parents in the better organisations were asked to fill in a form detailing what their home was like, their economic circumstances, and the contact details of two referees, which would be followed up by at least one home visit to verify what was said on the form. However, some societies did say that in 'special circumstances' some of these criteria would be overlooked. The laxity of some selection processes led to some very unfortunate mistakes in a society's choice of adoptive parent, as the committee was to report:

> *A child was placed with adopters without either an interview or a home visit and was handed over to the adoptive mother at a railway station. Her husband had described himself as a baker earning £150 per annum, and he gave a clergyman's reference which was duly obtained and was regarded as satisfactory. In consequence of complaints as to the treatment of the child, inquiries were made and it was found that the man's statement was false, and that he had been unemployed for some years. His character was unsatisfactory, and he is said to have taken the child around with him while he hawked produce stolen from allotments. The society's representative admitted in evidence that the man had adopted the child for the purpose of exploiting it as an object of sympathy by taking it around with his barrow. In these circumstances it was necessary to remove the child.*

This was not the only example of inappropriate choice of adoptive parents. One little girl was inadvertently (because insufficient checks were made) placed in a home where the couple were experiencing problems with their marriage. The husband started staying away from home at night, leaving the child with neighbours; he then assaulted his wife who left him, abandoning her new daughter.

In 1933, a man known locally to have a drink problem was arrested for theft. It transpired that he had two adopted children. His wife, who was elderly, had lied about her age on the application form and proved to be completely unsuitable to be responsible for the care of two young children.

Another little girl was placed with a blind man and his wife. The man was in receipt of a pension of ten shillings (approximately £73 today), which he added to by hawking and taking in lodgers. The adoptive mother died in 1934, and the girl, now 15 years old, was still sleeping in her father's bedroom; in December 1934, one of the lodgers was convicted of having sexual relations with the girl.

Another child was placed with a woman with mental health issues, who was not fit to look after the child, yet the adoptive mother had provided a reference from a probation officer. Another adoption society successively placed four children with a completely unsuitable home where at least one of the children was ill-treated; all of the children had to be removed, and the secretary for the adoption society admitted to the committee that they should never have placed children in this home in the first place. Finally, another child was placed with a couple who were dependent upon unemployment benefit and Poor Law relief; eight weeks after the adoption the father was placed in the local mental hospital as he was suffering from general paralysis of the insane (a brain disorder caused by untreated late-stage syphilis).

The Committee sadly noted that there were many examples of poor judgement when it came to the choice of adoptive parents, and in their recommendations they put forward in strong terms the clear need for meticulous procedures for would-be adoptive parents. These should include compulsory application forms, and checks on the income and state of health of the applicants. Visits to the applicant's house would assess the home the adopted child would grow up in, and for each child to be adopted, at least three interviews with the assigned case worker were recommended.

Another practice which came to light during the Committee's investigations was the payments made by the birth mother to the adoption societies. While some societies did not ask for any payments from the birth mother, in others it was common practice for them to ask the mother to contribute towards the upkeep of her baby in their care and also to pay towards the administration costs of the adoption itself. One society told the Committee that it asked for ten shillings per week for three months after the adoption, and also required an annual inspection fee of £1.00. One society asked for ten shillings per week; another, weekly payments up to a total amount of £60 or 5s a week for two years – this is despite the fact that even the best adoption societies could arrange and supervise an adoption for less than £9 in 1935. Societies asking for these amounts stated that they were for out-of-pocket and overhead expenses, plus supervision costs for the adopted child up to the age of 16. However, such supervision was not actually carried out.

The mothers who were asked for these amounts were sometimes required to enter into a written agreement, whereas in other societies the agreement was verbal and voluntary. What is disturbing about these payments is that they are being asked for at an extremely vulnerable moment in a woman's life and it appears to have been in contravention of the agreement signed by a mother when she handed over a baby – the agreement in which the adoption society clearly states that they will make 'no claim against the mother or any other person whatsoever'. What compounds it is the report that some mothers were vigorously pursued for the payments if they fell into arrears, even though there was no formal agreement. They were even threatened with legal proceedings if they did not bring their payments up to date. Other mothers continued to make maintenance payments for their baby even though it had been adopted and was with new parents – the adoption society did not tell them this had taken place, so that she would know to stop the payments.

It is hardly surprising that one of the societies with aggressive payment collection methods took steps to alter them during the course of the Committee's enquiries, changing their reminder letters to the mother to ones of persuasion rather than threats. Changes to the payment methods were also implemented – no doubt they were only too aware that they came across as draconian. The Committee did state that they had no problem with the mother contributing towards costs. They thought payment was a good idea: 'She should be reminded of her responsibilities, and ... the impression should not be cultivated that adoption societies exist for the cheap and expeditious disposal of illegitimate children.'

Another practice that drew criticism was the method used to conceal the identity and whereabouts of the adoptive parents from the birth mother. This seems to have been partly in response to the general feeling that the 'best' adoptive parents would want complete separation from the birth parents and indeed, there were instances of adoptive parents moving into another area in order to ensure privacy and to reduce the possibility of the birth mother turning up on the doorstep and not only embarrassing them, but also revealing to the neighbours that they had an adopted child. In order to hang on to 'quality' adoptive parents, keep the birth mother at a distance when it comes to information about the adoptive family, and also reduce the possibility of proceedings being held up because the birth mother had disappeared, she was often asked to sign a blank form which did not include any details of the new family.

Other stories related how the adoptive family's details were covered up while the birth mother signed the agreement, so she could not see it, or putting the adoptive family's address as 'care of' the adoption society, to conceal their whereabouts from the mother. Another tactic was to fail to reveal to the guardian *ad litem* – the representative who acted for the child in the adoption – the birth mother's address, so that her wishes could not be voiced. The motives for this seemingly shabby treatment of some birth mothers seem to have been largely unfounded.

The Chief Education Officer for Birmingham reported that out of 120 adoptions, for example, on only three occasions did a birth mother make a nuisance of herself. It seems that little consideration was given to the deep-seated need of the mother to know what had happened to her baby, even if only to know she or he was 'happy', and it is reinforced in the report that a mother could enquire as to her baby's welfare up to the point of adoption only, but not after that time.

Another aspect of adoption highlighted by the Horsbrugh Report was the adoption overseas of British children. This was a practice deliberated on by Miss Horsbrugh and her colleagues, and their conclusion was that the adoption of children to British nationals who happened to live abroad could not be stopped because one could not prevent a British person adopting a British child purely because of an accident of address. In the years prior to the report, children had been sent from adoption societies to adoptive parents in Holland, France, Belgium, Switzerland, Norway and the USA. Holland was a 'popular' destination and it was often to Dutch families that such children went, as Holland had no provision for adoption at all, although there was some unease in the Dutch authorities as the influx of adoptive children from abroad seemed to undermine their institutional opposition to the concept of adoption.

Numerous accounts over the years of the perils of adopting children out of the country are recounted. In one case, the illegitimate son of a 'high class' Englishwoman was placed in the Netherlands with an adoptive family of equal social standing to her own. The birth father had agreed to pay enough to cover the boy's education till he reached the age of 16, but when he reached his seventeenth birthday the payments stopped. Astonishingly, even though they had had the boy all those years, his adoptive family returned him to England; the teenager spoke no English and did not even know he was a British subject. A similar case originated in Germany in 1935, when a young man of 24 was deported from Germany to Britain, as he had become chargeable to the German relief system. It transpired that he had been adopted to a family in Germany from England at the age of three. Again, he spoke no English and it must have been a deeply upsetting experience to be removed from the culture he had grown up in, and effectively 'abandoned' in what was to him a foreign country.

In 1934, a girl was sent by an adoption society to adopters in Ceylon (now Sri Lanka), but was soon returned by them – apparently she was 'mentally abnormal' (these words verbatim from the report, and not elaborated on by the Committee) and should never have been sent out in the first place. Indeed, this little girl does not sound like the type of child the adoption societies would put forward at this time for adoption anyway. However, her disability is no excuse for the fact that she was dispatched back to England in a neglected state and poor physical condition.

Clearly, sending small children long distances to foreign countries, where the culture and even the nationality of the new family might be different to their own, must have been traumatic for them. Despite this, adoption societies in this era claimed that they only supplied children to high class families abroad, but it must have been extremely difficult to make adequate checks on families who were many hundreds or thousands of miles away.

Despite the fact that the societies also claimed that there was such demand from abroad for children that they could not fulfil the demand, the Committee was dubious about the practice of adopting children out of the country, and recommended that although they could be adopted to British nationals because 'to place children with such persons is not to transplant them into an alien community', they must not be adopted out to foreign nationals and children should only be adopted out to British nationals if the adoption was going to be a legal one and not de facto, that is, in practice only or informal.

Another feature of adoptions at this time was again highlighted by the Committee, and that was the private or independent adoption agent. Some private agents are obvious choices – the sympathetic midwife, doctor or welfare worker who wanted to help the mother adopt her baby as quickly and discreetly as possible, so avoiding any possible public exposure or extended period of waiting; other individuals made a business out of the process of adoption for personal gain. One case concerned a woman known as 'Mrs A', who acted as a third party for profit in nine adoptions in the South of England in the early 1930s. She placed advertisements in the newspapers for the babies she was looking to place, for example:

> *I's a lovely baby boy. I'm lonely and sad without mummy*
> *and daddy to make me glad; will anyone adopt me?*
> *Write box ....*
> *Good refined home wanted for Army Officer's twin boy*
> *and girl, fortnight old. Write Box ....*

The 'broker' also answered advertisements placed by couples looking to adopt a child, or advertisements from birth parents looking to have a baby adopted. However she made contact with birth or potential adoptive parents, it was she who arranged the adoptions, not only of children who came direct from the birth family, but also of those children who had been placed with her as a foster parent.

It was a lucrative trade, or as the committee put it, 'cases of a very serious character, involving what can only be described as trafficking in children'. Mrs A received £40 to £50 from the birth mother, although she later claimed under oath that she had taken as little as £5 which barely covered her expenses. She was eventually charged in 1932 with three separate charges under Part 1 of the Children Act 1908, for failing to give notice to the local authority within 48 hours of the reception of an infant under seven years of age. When her house was inspected, it was found to be dirty and unacceptable, with four foster children living there. Mrs A was in touch with the mothers of the children, and typically had taken a large down payment from them – in one case £44 for helping with the birth of the baby, and adoption fee – but pestered this particular mother for a further £10.

Another woman who ran a nursing home used for the confinements of single mothers, was found to have been paying people to adopt children – one man living on unemployment assistance was paid £30 each to legally adopt two children this way, which implies that the woman had received considerably more than that in payment from the birth mother. She reported to the local authority the placing of 50 illegitimate children with foster parents, and for at least 22 of these she had received lump sum payments. This woman was also involved in the placement of babies not born in her nursing home, and in one case gave an adoptive parent £50 to take the child.

Finally, there was a bizarre case, which can only be thought of as the 'hoarding' of children. A woman who lived with her mother, with very limited income, used several aliases and posed as a comfortably off married woman. Between 1927 and 1930, she managed to adopt five children and would have kept a sixth, had it not been for the second thoughts of the father who reclaimed the child. She would repeatedly leave home for a while and let it be known that she was going to a nursing home – and return with yet another baby which she claimed was her own. Her house was dirty and overcrowded and sadly three of 'her' children died as a result. It is difficult with hindsight to say if this woman was suffering from any form of mental illness, but had she tried to adopt through one of the major adoption societies, it is highly unlikely she would have been accepted.

It is hardly surprising that Miss Horsbrugh's Committee concluded 'We think it is dangerous to permit private persons to receive payments for arranging adoptions'. They recommended using the deterrent of criminal proceedings and the intervention of the court when any payment of this kind was mooted.

The 13 recommendations made by Miss Horsbrugh's Committee are a direct result of what they heard and read during their sojourn. For example, they had been deeply impressed by the excellence of the procedures undertaken by the London County Council during their adoption arrangements, and many of their recommendations followed on from this: thorough and consistent screening of both birth and adoptive parents prior to adoption going ahead; a mandatory probation period of at least three months; and an insistence on application to the courts for an adoption at the end of the probationary period. Hostels were to be of a decent standard, and staff should be suitably qualified.

The issue of adopting children out of the country to foreign nationals was also addressed, as were payments to private persons for arranging an adoption. These recommendations were to form the basis of future legislation, but were criticised because they did not call for the banning of private adoptions (although strictly speaking, the Committee's brief was to examine the practices of adoption societies first and foremost). Many of its recommendations became part of Miss Horsbrugh's Adoption of Children (Regulation) Bill in 1939, which became law before the war but did not come into effect until 1943.

On the Eve of War
Just before the declaration of war in September 1939, the NCUMC came of age, and its Chairman, Mrs Fisher, was in a quietly celebratory mood. She wrote about the work done to bring down death rates among illegitimate babies, which had fallen since the end of the First World War in 1918 – at their height it had been over 200 per thousand births and dropped over the intervening years to 88 per thousand just before the war in 1939.

Great strides had been made in improving mother and baby homes and the networks of welfare workers available to help the unmarried mother. The maximum amount payable under an affiliation order had risen from five shillings to £1 (20 shillings) and collection methods were more successful. Of course, all this was part of the work of the NCUMC to keep mother and baby together, which was felt by the organisation to be much less injurious to both of them in the long run – for example, it avoided the pain of a child endlessly wondering why they had been given up by their birth mother and, in those days, rarely having the chance to obtain answers. It is relevant, however, because without their work, the number of babies waiting for adoption would have been much higher, and the NCUMC could be said to have established a precedent for the later norm of the family staying together with the full support of the state.

There still remained many children for whom adoptive parents had not come forward, however, and the agencies concerned with their care did their best to place them in kindly foster homes as the next best thing. The Waifs and Strays Home of 'Holy Innocents' in Bath was actively campaigning in 1939 for foster parents to volunteer to care for the 17 'toddlers' aged between 18 months and five years in the home. The hope was that if foster parents and child developed a bond, then an adoption would then follow. The *Bath Chronicle and Weekly Gazette* did its best to promote the cause with an article specially designed to tug at the heart strings:

> *These little foster children are bringing happiness and brightness to many childless homes, and companionship and interest where there was loneliness before. They have seldom known the love of parents, and some have been rendered homeless and orphaned. Happy and well cared for, as they are in the Society's homes, when they grow older they long for and miss the individual love and attention ... If there are any readers who feel they would like to give their love to, and mother one of these little ones, who long to call someone Mummy, or better still married couples, so they may have a Daddy, too, will they please write to us?*

It is also made clear that at the age of five, if no one has come forward as foster parents, the children have to be moved to a residential home for older children.

It was also stipulated in the article that applicants should be full members of the Church of England and if a married couple, they should have no children at all and certainly none under the age of seven. In return, the foster family received eight shillings (the equivalent of approximately £52 today) per week and the child would arrive at their new home with a complete new set of clothes. It would undoubtedly be to everyone's benefit if the child was adopted by the new family, as the Waifs and Strays would then not have to pay the fostering fee, the child had permanency, and the new parents would have a longed-for child of their own. This is an interesting article in that it confirms that single people were welcomed as foster and adoptive parents.

This article is also in puzzling contrast to the upbeat news from the NCAA who, in 1935, were happily stating that they had more potential adoptive families on their books than they had children available. It would seem that adoptive parents may have been more choosy than many charities cared to admit, and that very young babies remained the child of choice for most adoptive parents.

At the end of the 1930s, charitable organisations were still growing in influence and profile. By 1939, the NSPCC had helped an estimated 5,000,000 children, while in 1930, the National Children's Home had over 4,000 children in its care across 31 local or regional centres. Of these, 600 children were boarded out with foster parents, and it was the charity's proud claim that overall, 500 of their charges had been adopted out over the years.

National Baby Week was still an annual event, and in 1939 it promoted a pamphlet by Dr Dennis Geffen entitled *Aspects of Fathercraft*, giving advice to would-be fathers. The expectant father was urged to do his bit while his wife awaited the birth of the baby. While the mother to be was filling in the months before the birth by quietly crafting the baby's layette, father should be washing down paintwork or decorating to make himself useful.

Once the baby had arrived he must never discourage his wife from feeding the baby herself, and if he was home from work early enough, must allow an hour in the evening to play with his baby. Furthermore, 'Fathers must realise that babies require peace and sufficient rest, and should not insist on having the wireless set blaring forth to the detriment of the child. It is harmful, moreover, for children to be in an atmosphere laden with tobacco fumes.' It would seem that the role and participation of the father was now being encouraged – up to a point.

World War Two
When war was declared on 3 September 1939, many Britons must have had a sinking feeling of déjà vu. Although not an exact repeat of the 1914–18 war, many tribulations faced the population and were similar to what families had gone through twenty years before. The heartache of losing loved ones; rationing of virtually everything from basic foodstuffs to clothes, fuel and furniture; disruption of bombings and damage to or loss of property; the displacement of individuals and entire families, were just a few of the major experiences people had to deal with.

However, many adults also experienced a new feeling of liberation and had the opportunity to see different countries, meet a much wider spectrum of people, and have a lifestyle they could never have dreamed of. One young man from the Midlands, brought up in a very large but terribly deprived family, only ate his first ever 'meat and two veg' dinner when he joined the Marines at the age of 18. He described his war experience (he was not injured) as the best time of his life, and he was not the only one to feel like this.

Other people discovered a new-found freedom – often away from spouses, family and watchful neighbours – to have relationships that would have been more difficult to start in the pre-war years. The top-right postcard on Plate 5 shows how deeply this new-found laissez-faire attitude to relationships was reflected in popular culture. Printed in Britain during the war, the postcard features a young woman firmly telling her beau on the telephone that marriage is not for her, and in the background is a 'rogue's gallery' of boyfriends – either former or current – who come from all the services and from 'civvie street' too. To the modern eye this young lady is pretty demure, with her knee-length frock and neat appearance.

However, to a 1940s person with a conservative outlook, this busy girlfriend is positively racy. She is shown lounging on a sofa, the tops of her legs tantalisingly on show, her under-slip evident, and the neckline of her close-fitting frock rather too low for respectability. Taken as a whole, the image is that of a good-time girl who had no intention of settling down, but who was intent on playing the field. Her left hand is covered so we don't know if she is married or not (it would have been a step too far to show a married woman multi-dating, or even dating at all, at the time, and regarded as very bad for morale), so the viewer is left to make up their own minds. This telling image says much about the new morality that many adults adopted with enthusiasm.

Many affairs began and ended during the war: married people whose spouses were away; war workers working long hours in the new company of fellow employees; single couples already courting but deciding to seize the day and have an affair or get married before one or both went off to the war, leading to more young widows with children than there would have been normally.

The arrival of the USA forces in Britain in 1942 brought an aura of Hollywood glamour and prosperity to ration-hit Brits and they were immensely popular dates, leading to the none-too-flattering catchphrase 'overpaid, oversexed and over here'. Stories of 'back home' fascinated their British girlfriends and families and generous gifts of chocolate, chewing gum, stockings and more added to their allure. Little wonder that 70,000 British girls became GI Brides, but that statistic does not include all the young women who merely had relationships with the American servicemen.

However, a sense of having to take happiness while one could inevitably led to mistakes, even recklessness, and the result was many more unwanted pregnancies, not just outside marriage but from married women too who were carrying the baby of their lover, not their spouse who was away at the war. Penelope, a young Liverpool woman, had an affair with a GI. It was a very typical story – bowled over by flattery, gifts and promises of marriage, she slept with him and became pregnant. She was fortunate in that her family supported her desire to keep the baby, perhaps as some compensation for being jilted by her lover, but also some members of the family were deeply scathing of her gullibility, a hostility that lasted well after the war with some individuals.

Penelope was accused of being a simpleton by some relatives for allowing herself to end up in this predicament, but she was resourceful enough to be able to keep and bring up her baby, working well into retirement age to keep a roof over their heads. Other women also became pregnant but refused to marry or be supported by their American partner, not wanting to leave home and family; they chose to go it alone and face the stigma of being a 'loose' woman – of course this also stigmatised the child as illegitimate as well.

It would be inaccurate, however, to suggest that the American soldiers were the only overseas visitors who fathered children. Shortly after the war, in 1946, B.E. Astbury, the General Secretary of the Family Welfare Association, wrote, 'One of the greatest social problems which six years of "occupation" by troops of all nationalities has left this country to grapple with is that of illegitimacy.'

Another problem caused within the British armed services was the increasing number of cases faced by Army Welfare Officers of babies born into the families of soldiers who were away on service. Under these circumstances it was sometimes suggested as an option to the soldiers concerned, that it might be better for the long-term happiness of the whole family unit that they accept the child as their own and carry on with married and family life. But that must have been a hard decision to take in those days. One also has to question why the Welfare Officers suggested it – perhaps it was seen as better for morale than for the soldier to be distracted by thoughts of divorce. Of course, those babies who would not be accepted would be adopted out at some point, or sadly, may have gone to live in children's homes.

By the end of the war, the illegitimacy rate had risen to 9 per cent: there were 63,420 illegitimate births registered in 1945, compared to 25,633 in 1939. This rise in more liberated behaviour, and its consequences, did not escape the scrutiny of various interested parties. In a speech at the annual meeting of the York Diocesan Maternity Home in May 1945, Dr Cyril Garbutt, the then Archbishop of York, aired his views on the matter of the unmarried mother, her baby, and the problems they presented to society. He stated that the moral laxity of the times was indeed due to the war, and considered the role of the Church in dealing with this unfortunate group of vulnerable people.

The Archbishop also deplored the rise in divorce and made a plea for more and better housing which would enhance family life; he then expounded the view that Christianity would be the saviour of the young single mother, giving her self-respect, new hope, and in turn, the baby would be brought up in a Christian environment. Amazingly, this point of view has strong echoes in the plea of Monsignor Nugent 40 years before; not much had changed in some regards.

It is hardly surprising that with the rise in illegitimate births, adoption rates rose too. In 1946, 21,280 children were adopted, compared to 6,832 in 1939, the figure having risen steadily over the course of the war.

Mass Observation

Some of the adoptions during 1939 to 1945 are vividly commented on in the Mass Observations Diaries. 'Mass Obs', as it is sometimes affectionately termed, was begun in 1937 as a form of 'anthropological study' of the British nation and people and is made up primarily of diaries and writings by individuals from all walks of life. It is particularly interesting as an insight into the freely offered opinions of ordinary people on the subjects of the day and would have been especially valuable to gauge morale during the 1939–45 war.

Some diarists, known primarily by their given MO number, do mention adoption, but in the cases examined, do not state if the babies adopted are the result of wartime liaisons or not. In fact, Diarist number 5399, a retired nurse aged 68 from Sussex, reflects in December 1944 on the recent adoption by her neighbours of a three-month-old baby girl. The adoptive father is a serving air force man and his wife is a homemaker, and the story is recounted as follows:

*Two of my neighbours, man and wife, and he is serving in the
Air Force, have adopted a three- month's [sic] baby girl. They
have been married seven years, and both want a child. She says,
even if she does have one of her own now, she doesn't care ...
They only got her last week, and she seems very good and very
contented. They say she is a war orphan, mother killed in an air
raid, and father died at the front. But I don't quite believe it.
However, it is the best sort of story to tell the child, if it is needed
later on. I think the woman is very brave to take it on now, and
so does the husband.*

If the delighted parents of this baby girl were keen to tell this particular
story of their daughter's short life so far, it is reasonable to deduce that
any alternative – such as that she is an illegitimate child – would be
unfavourably received by the wider world of family and community, and
the young couple may have been subjected to dire warnings about the
dangers of taking on a child with 'bad blood'. Clearly the age of the sins
of the mother being visited on the child, had not yet passed.

Diarist number 5460, a young woman from Newport in
Monmouthshire who worked as a railway clerk, excitedly recounts her
application to adopt a baby in 1944/5, and frets over the problems of
gathering baby Katherine's layette together within the restrictions of
rationing (which were particularly tiresome and restrictive by the end of
the war). Her husband, Diarist number 5233, who was a radio operator
among other jobs, takes a much more sentimental view of the adoption
than his wife, perhaps because he did not have the worries of managing
the rations and baby's clothing coupons.

Diarist number 5256, a female infant school teacher in her thirties from
Manchester, describes the tribulations of her friend Ena, who was trying to
adopt, and also records the arrival of the baby, whom the diarist describes
as 'very solemn and unnaturally good'. Today, such quietude in a young
baby might ring alarm bells in social workers and health professionals as it
did with the diarist, and it is tempting to wonder if the baby had had a very
unsettled start in life; but one may never know the truth.

Another diarist (number 5003), a young man in his thirties, worked
as a commercial artist and gardener in Kent and lodged with a family
which included a 20-year-old daughter. To his astonishment, the diarist
finds out that the daughter had had a baby out of wedlock at the age of 17

– in approximately 1938. Apparently, while she was pregnant, she had to give up her work very early on and conceal the pregnancy as far as was possible at the insistence of her mother.

The expectant teenage mother had to stay in the house nearly all of the time, and was only allowed for walks after dark and in the company of her mother. The baby was adopted six weeks after birth by 'posh people'. It sounds odd to a modern reader that the young woman had her life so severely restricted by her family in order to protect their good name, but even more surprising is the diarist's reaction to the news. He is hugely shocked to hear that the girl had gone off the rails like this and wrote 'It's going to take me a bit of time to get over the news!'

He goes on to make this rather shallow remark, comparing the daughter and a young woman named Yvonne whom he greatly admired: 'To think that this kid is a mother ... Yvonne practically radiates "it" and yet she keeps men at a distance. Yet — who possesses very little sex attraction was a mother when she was seventeen!' Clearly this young man was subconsciously making assumptions about the 'type' of girl who 'would' and was assuming that they would have to be extremely attractive to tempt a fellow to go that far – one can only assume he had had a rather sheltered life!

Although this young man was commenting on an illegitimate birth that happened before the war, his words are, unfortunately, very representative of many people right through this period. Despite the *carpe diem* attitude which prevailed in the war, opinions about young women who had children out of wedlock were not much better than they had always been.

Thankfully, some people took a less condemnatory approach. In 1944, Diarist number 5337, a housewife in her early sixties, was engaged in various community and social action projects, one of which was to support a single mother through the process of giving up her baby for adoption. This diarist's tone is much gentler:

> *Went down to ... see a girl who has got an illegitimate baby she wants adopted. Such a pretty girl, a mere child of 18. Poor little Thing evidently it is going to be an awful struggle to part with the baby. Told her I would write to the Adoption Soc. and help all I can. She comes from Wales and has been here hidden away ... Has no friends she says here, said I would send her books etc.*

A week later, on Armistice Day (11 November), this empathetic lady was helping the single Mum to fill in forms 'about the adoption of the baby, with the girl, she is so pretty, and so good about it all, filled up the form most sensibly and well. I do hope it will go through quickly for her, as I feel every day she has the baby it makes it more hard for her to part with it.'

Events took an unexpected turn towards the end of the month, to the qualified relief of the diarist:

Went down ... on my bike to see the girl as she had written to me saying after all a relation was going to adopt it. When I got there I found her looking so happy, and after all she is going to keep the baby herself, Mother and 'Uncle' have apparently come round, Father is abroad, and doesn't seem to have been consulted. However I am very glad as she evidently adored it, only hope she gets married soon.

This is a charming yet poignant story, and illustrates that even though there was an overall antipathy to single mothers and their children on a societal level right through the period looked at, there were also plenty of people who felt sympathy for mother and baby, and others who, for whatever reason, were able to see a need for pragmatic support. This baby, born in 1944, was just one of 55,173 babies registered as being born outside marriage, from a total of 751,478 birth registrations in total – it sounds an insignificant percentage, yet it was more than double the figure from 1939 (25,570). The following year it reached a wartime high of 63,420 – little wonder that there was a post-war 'adoption boom', with the greater numbers of illegitimate babies needing new families, although, as this last story shows, some babies remained, we hope happily, with their mother and extended family.

One curiosity of the war years was the rise in the number of people who came forward wanting to adopt baby girls rather than boys. In a letter to *The Times* of 21 August 1945, Leonora Jenner, the Chair of the Western National Adoption Society, highlighted this anomaly and said that, whereas they had a waiting list of baby boys looking for homes, they had a waiting list of adoptive parents waiting for baby girls. She reinforced the fact that 'All these babies come from well recommended, normally respectable mothers, are all first illegitimate children and the health and parentage have been investigated and a satisfactory blood test has been obtained ... The average is two to six months.'

Yet again, there is a hint of the Victorian notion that only women who were respectable and had made just the one 'slip' were the best providers of a potentially adoptable child. Perhaps there was still a fear that to take the babies of a habitually 'loose' woman was to encourage her immorality, whereas to take the baby of a respectable woman who had made a one-off mistake was to do genuine good work. Opinions on those who stood outside the perceived moral norms still changed very slowly indeed.

Evacuation

Other families expanding as a result of taking children in were those which offered billets to evacuees. The great evacuation, which had been carefully rehearsed beforehand, began on 1 September 1939, two days before the declaration of war, and during 'Operation Pied Piper' as it was known, official statistics tell us that more than 1,500,000 people were moved to places of safety. This included over 800,000 children of school age, more than half a million mothers with young children, and approximately 13,000 pregnant women, many of whom would have given birth to their babies in their new location.

Those who took the children in were paid a small amount for doing so (10s 6d, the equivalent of £67.92) but often complained bitterly that it was not enough, especially with the added costs of buying the children better clothes, the higher food bill, and extra laundry where a child was stressed by the move and began bed wetting. In North Wales, organisers kept a stock of items available for loan to ease the pressure on the sometimes reluctant foster parents – everything from mattresses, blankets and treasure cots to pie dishes, tea spoons, arm chairs, scrubbing brushes and zinc bath tubs could be loaned out. Some of the evacuated children were treated like the householder's own children, loved and nurtured, and indeed never went home again, much preferring the family that had taken them in.

Other children fared less well – as Mass Observation Diarist 5337 reported, 'Mrs White ... says that the little evacuees next door to her are still not well treated.' Eight days later, the diarist was relieved to report that the children had returned to their own family in London. In fact, a substantial number of children returned home shortly after being evacuated – by the beginning of 1940, something like a million evacuees, including many children, had returned home, as the immediate threat of bombings and invasion seemed to dissipate. For parents in vulnerable urban areas who had had their children removed from happy, close-knit homes – a form of forced fostering – it could come as a terrible shock. One young woman who worked in a munitions factory in Birmingham in 1941/2 vividly remembered the distress that one of her workmates felt at having her two-year-old son evacuated to the countryside.

We worked long hours and it wasn't easy to get away to see your children – travelling wasn't easy and she only saw her little boy every few weeks. She was in a terrible state. I remember her sitting opposite me at the work table – we were supposed to be inspecting tiny springs to go in the cannon of a Bristol Beaufighter [heavy bomber plane] – and just sobbing all the time, she couldn't stop crying. She couldn't see to do her job either! In the end she couldn't stand it any more and brought him back to Brum. She said they would take their chances together.

Other experiences were more positive: from one Birkenhead family, the mother and three daughters were all evacuated to Hawarden in North Wales in the early 1940s as part of a later wave of evacuations prompted by the threat of bombing at the Birkenhead docks. The mother and youngest child, barely a toddler, went to one house where mother worked as housekeeper, and the two older children aged approximately 12 and 6 found themselves billeted at the vicarage, after a less than enthusiastic reception at the home of a single lady in the village.

As Eleanor, the oldest girl recounted:

The Vicarage had a long sweeping drive up to the big black and white mock Tudor house, which all the visitors used, but we children had to use the back door into the kitchen. We were not allowed in the library but we did play in the garden a lot; it sloped down to a little wood with a stream and we took the Vicar's Corgi dog down there. We all went in the stream and got the dog very muddy which wasn't really allowed, so we had to try to clean him up before we went back in the house! The Vicar also used to walk into the village with us, wearing his long black clerical cloak. If he wanted to cross the main street he would step out into the road and hold up his arm for the cars to stop! We children loved that, I think he just did it to amuse us as it was a quiet village. He was a very nice man. Another person I met in the village was a very eccentric lady from the big house. She stopped and talked to me and when she found out I was living at the vicarage, she said she would send over an old tea set for us to play with. It arrived in a big tea chest and as I was happily unpacking it, the Vicar's wife saw it and said 'Oh my goodness, you can't play with that! It is far too good for you to play with.' So it was taken off us. I don't think the eccentric lady was meant to send it to us after all, as it was so valuable.

The children's stay at the vicarage was overall very happy and a far cry from the endangered terraced streets and docks of Birkenhead. Other stories include the Christmas parties at the 'big house', with fancy dress and prizes, meeting up with Mother and the baby sister (who lived at the other end of the village) periodically, and Dad cycling all the way from Birkenhead one day for a visit, complete with new black patent shoes for Eleanor.

The children in this case possibly had the best of both worlds, continued contact with parents but also benevolent foster parents. Add to this the fact that after two years the family returned to Birkenhead as the threat of blitz was thought to be receding, and one can see that these girls always understood that foster 'parents' did not replace one's own family. For young children who were sent many miles from their families and who never received visits or many communications, the distinction would have been much less clear as time went by.

Morale-building encouragement for the foster parents of evacuees continued throughout the war. In March 1942, the School Medical Officer of Bridgwater stated that 'a word of praise is due to the foster parents, who in the early months of the war, looked after these children, but who, with the prolongation of hostilities, are now literally bringing up these children, often in the face of extreme difficulties'. When war ended, some children even stayed with their foster parents, such was the bond that had developed between them in often trying circumstances.

Some evacuees came from much farther afield. On 25 November

1938, less than a year before war was declared, a radio appeal was put out via the BBC Home Service to the British public. Foster homes were urgently required for children – mainly Jewish – under the age of 17 (some only infants) who were part of an emergency evacuation from Europe to England, known as the Kindertransport.

It was known that Jewish families were now suffering under the Nazi regime led by Adolf Hitler, but the call to action followed the events of Kristallnacht on 9 and 10 November 1938 when many Jewish-owned buildings, businesses and synagogues were attacked and damaged or destroyed. The British Government was persuaded to allow the most threatened children to travel to Britain on the basis that they would return to their parents when the situation had settled down; they also each had to have a £50 (nearly £7,000 in today's money) bond from a sponsor to ensure their ultimate resettlement.

A team of people ranging from secular supporters to those from many different religious denominations worked to gather the children together, and place them on sealed trains, and from there the children travelled to the sea port of Harwich, the first arriving on 2 December 1938 – there were approximately 200 children who had been moved away not only from their families, but from their home country as well. Between that date and the departure of the last of the Kindertransport, some 10,000 children were evacuated from mainland Europe. Ironically, the last group left on 1 September 1939, the day when Operation Pied Piper – the mass evacuation of British children from at risk areas into the countryside – began.

The Kindertransport children were dispersed to pre-arranged accommodation, approximately half of them to foster homes of varying quality and levels of affection, and others to country encampments run by Jewish youth movements, hostels, and farms across Britain. Presumably, some had similar experiences to the British-born children also evacuated away from their families, the biggest and most poignant difference being that most of the Kindertransport children were never to see their parents again – despite the £50 bond, they mostly had no family to go back to at the end of the war.

The Times newspaper reported on a group of 46 Jewish Kindertransport children who arrived in Southampton on 30 December 1938 on the American liner *Washington*: 'They ranged in age from 3 years to 17 and were mostly from Berlin. Some are going to friends and relatives who have already settled in England; others will be taken into English families ... The older ones will be given vocational training to prepare them for settlement overseas.'

Of the previous 1,550 Kindertransport children brought into Britain, the article reported: 'The holiday camp at Dovercourt has proved satisfactory, and the children there are happy and well. Others have gone to hostels and homes at Broadstairs, Felixstowe, Harwich, and Walton-on-the-Naze.'

The article concluded by pointing out that 'Legal adoption of foreign children is not permissible'. This is one crucial difference between these children, so far from home and family, compared to the vast majority of the other children in foster care in England and Wales at the time, including 'native' evacuees – they could not be adopted and become a permanent part of any family. They had arrived in England as guests on the clear understanding that at some point they would return home; this, of course, was to prove a false hope.

The other alternative was that they should move on at the age of 18, but there were plenty of observers who wanted to keep and nurture these young people as assets to the nation. One letter to *The Times* newspaper even suggested an amendment to the 1926 Adoption of Children Act so that these children could indeed be absorbed into British families. This correspondent wrote in 1939, 'The children we are educating at present are the pick of Germany and Austria. Cannot we make use of these brilliant youngsters who are full of gratitude to the country which saved them? An amendment of the act referred to so that these children may become full British citizens would be a blessing to them and a great advantage to England.'

By 1946, many thousands of the evacuated children had, however, been happily reunited with their birth families, although the bonds of affection and loyalty to the foster families continued for a lifetime as well. Some children were never to go home; also in 1946, the influential Curtis Report noted in that of 100,000 in the care of institutions, 5,000 of these were homeless evacuees.

Helping the Unmarried Mother
Despite the tribulations of wartime, the attentions of moral welfare workers continued to focus on the unmarried mothers and their babies. A disturbing newspaper report in the *Bath Chronicle and Weekly Gazette*

on 2 December 1944 begins by outlining the efforts of various agencies in the city to establish a hostel for mothers to go to after their illegitimate babies are born. This was fully supported by the Western National Adoption Society, which supported the project as they saw a need for accommodation for the mothers and their babies to go until an adoption could be arranged. The Honourable Secretary, Mrs Moss-Blundell, said, 'A hostel is a crying need in this city' and added that with the rate of illegitimate births having doubled, the society was receiving 'a tremendous number of applications for adoption'.

So far, so good – until the section of the report which states that the National Children Adoption Society claimed that baby farms were thriving despite the Adoption Act, and that the only thing that would end the evil of baby farming was decent mother and baby hostels. It was probably inevitable that some people would take advantage of the renewed crisis of lone mothers and babies and step into the breach that the authorities had yet to fill.

Despite the advent of war, attention was given to improving adoption legislation. In 1943, the Adoption of Children Regulation Act came into full operation on 1 June, in order to regularise, limit and strengthen the position of the adoption societies.

CHAPTER 5

For the Welfare of All Concerned
1945–1961

Just as the laissez-faire attitudes towards relationships in the First World War were mirrored by events of the Second World War, so was a rise in the divorce rate. However, during and after the 1939–45 war, the rise was much more dramatic than before.

Divorce rates had steadily risen over the interwar period and by 1939 had reached 8,254. Over the course of the war, rates rose steadily apart from a slight dip in 1941 and finished in 1945 at 15,634. In 1946 it had risen to 29,829, but in 1947, by the time most servicemen and women had been demobbed and were trying to rebuild their relationships, the divorce rate was an astonishing 60,254.

The 1939–45 war had revolutionised the way many people viewed their lives and their relationships and divorce was becoming less of a stigma, but also they were becoming less tolerant of the idea that all marriages should be adhered to, regardless of how one felt about it. Although the divorce rate fell steadily after this high, it began to rise sharply again in the 1960s, and in 1969 had reached 51,310. Divorce as a way of resolving marital conflict was now a regular feature of adult life, and with divorce came the single parent.

The Brave New World of the Welfare State
One beacon of light in the austere post-war years with their continued rationing, housing shortages and families striving to adjust to civilian life again, was the implementation of the National Health Service which began on 5 July 1948. For the first time, health care and other services were free to all regardless of social or monetary status – including maternity and antenatal services. This was to have important long-term significance for all women as time went by.

The National Health Service was only part of the revolution in the care of the nation during the post-war years, originally conceived by the Liberal politician William Beveridge, and implemented by the post-war Labour Government. The 1948 National Assistance Act formally abolished the hated and feared Poor Law system and replaced it with a social security system that would be much more familiar to the reader of the twenty-first century. The Act established a safety net for people who had not or could not pay National Insurance contributions (a system set up by two previous Acts of Parliament in 1946) and its categories included the homeless, the disabled and – crucially – unmarried mothers.

Under the Act, local Councils would now establish mother and baby homes for unmarried women before and after the birth of their baby, and some went further and also set up hostels for working mothers, to continue the help until the single mother could be independent and still support her baby.

As well as the National Health Service, legislation was being brought in after 1945 to support families with children. The Family Allowances Act of 1945 introduced regular payments for children, but not the oldest child.

Another Act of Parliament made its appearance in 1948: the Children's Act. Based on the highly influential report of the Child Care Committee chaired by Dame Myra Curtis, its focus was the treatment of children who were 'deprived of a normal home life' and who had been placed not only in public institutions, but also those run by charities. The report Dame Myra oversaw was criticised for being too dismissive of the most negative witness statements the Committee heard, but it did highlight various adverse aspects of children's care in institutions, such as the cold and informal way they were received into a children's home, poor and inadequate staffing, and inadequate accommodation and equipment.

According to the report, a lack of empathy, time and attention to the emotional well-being of these children was at the heart of the problem and could lead to behavioural issues and even poor development. The children the Committee members looked at came from a wide spectrum of backgrounds – juvenile offenders who were in local authority care; those with disabilities of all kinds; war orphans and evacuees who, for whatever reason, could not return home; and children who were under local authority care because they had been put into foster care, or put up for adoption.

This last group was growing, of course, because of the increase in illegitimate births during and immediately after the 1939–45 war. The Children's Act itself placed responsibility for the care of such children under the age of 17 firmly with local authorities, and also set the pattern for trained social workers to take on the work of looking after the children in care. Overall control was to rest with one government ministry. Finding homes and families for children was therefore considered vital wherever possible, and in her book, *Adoption in the Modern World*, published in 1952, Margaret Kornitzer quoted the following extract from the report which with great seriousness of tone, sets out this standpoint:

> *We wish to emphasise the extreme seriousness of taking a child away from even an indifferent home. The aim must be to find something better – even if it takes the responsibility of providing a substitute home. The methods which should be available may be treated under three main heads of adoption, boarding out and residence in communities. We have placed these in the order in which they seem to us to secure the welfare and happiness of the child.*

Consequently, children who had no family home of their own would now, for preference, be placed in foster homes rather than in institutional care in order to give them the closest possible experience to a 'normal' family life, and there was to be a greater emphasis on adoption where appropriate. Local authorities were to keep close watch on children fostered out to paid fosterers and also took responsibility for the registration of adoption societies. As a result, the number of children 'boarded out' or fostered rose steadily over the next 15 years, an increase of 17 per cent.

The Children's Act was in some ways very typical of the post-war optimism and drive towards an overall support for family and children, and there was a new determination to see children as individuals even though they were part of a 'system'. There has been debate as to whether it was successful. However, the intention to see children placed in family homes, to treat them with respect and due regard for their own personalities, must have alleviated the lonely wait of some children hoping for a new family to come and adopt them.

In 1950, a new Adoption Act was implemented to amend and

improve the existing legislation. Henceforward, a probationary period of three months had to be completed before the adoption order was granted to the adoptive parents, and a birth mother could not consent to the adoption of her baby until the child was at least six weeks old – to give the mother time to think through the consequences of giving her baby away.

In addition, the birth mother was now required to give consent to specific applicants (although they were not identified by name unless they wished to be so; normally a serial number was used on the paperwork instead). Another loose end was tied up with the regulation stating that an adopted child was to inherit only from their new parents just as if they were the parent's natural child. The investment made by the establishment in adoption through these two Acts gives a strong message that adoption was a process worth supporting.

The 1950s began as a decade of austerity and ended as a decade for some of slowly increasing prosperity and optimism. The new National Health Service was transforming the lives of poor and low income families, opening up a wide range of health services for women who had often lived for years with, for example, the ill-effects of bad teeth, poor vision, and ongoing problems caused by childbirth. The NHS also made it possible for all women to be attended by professionals paid for by the state, and to have free antenatal care such as check-ups and dental treatment.

Most women who gave birth before the advent of the National Health Service relied on relatives, neighbours, and only what professional health care could be afforded. Now, a woman giving birth at home could rely on the expert help of a fully qualified midwife, and if needs be she had a free bed waiting for her at the local maternity hospital.

However, it was also an era of continuing ignorance about the facts of life and parents did not help matters by keeping their sons and daughters in that state. In Lancashire, one young woman about to get married in the mid-1950s asked her mother what she could expect on her wedding night, as she knew nothing about the mechanics of sex and about how babies happened. 'All I will say is, what goes up, must come down', her mother cryptically replied. Needless to say, the new bride became pregnant not long after her honeymoon.

Little wonder that many young unmarried women found themselves pregnant after an affair, if they were not equipped with knowledge or supplies that could protect them from conception, and the debate over the moral, theological and cultural impact of widening access to contraception continued to rage.

In 1949 the Chairman and President of the Family Planning Association engaged in a debate about the subject with the church-based Mothers Union who questioned the morality of family planning. The Chairman wrote of relieving of pressure on families, especially the mother, who was compelled to have babies one after the other – sometimes, even, one per year – which would inevitably undermine the quality of life of the whole family unit.

The Royal Commission on Population also joined the public debate, stating their conviction that if safe and correct forms of contraception were not available, 'other means would be used; and some of them eg. criminal abortion, the prevalence of which even now is distressingly high, are very undesirable'. The Catholic women's organisations blamed not only the spread of contraceptive use, but also the rise of divorce for undermining traditional family life. By contrast, the Chair and Secretary of the Bradford Marriage Guidance Council stated, 'Is right ever achieved by withholding knowledge? People to-day are wrecking their nerves or their health, and sometimes disrupting their marriages because of wrong or ignorant use of contraceptives, or because of attempted abortions.'

For the organisations and public bodies, which took a pragmatic approach to family limitation, it must have seemed like a very slow path to changing the hearts of those morally opposed to it. Nevertheless, it is telling that there is no mention at all at this point in the public debates, of the single woman, or of the unmarried mother, who was probably the most vulnerable of them all. That would have been a step too far at this point in the dialogue, even though privately many commentators knew how important it was. Unsurprisingly there were still more than enough babies and small children available for adoptive parents to choose from.

The Adoption 'Boom'
After 1945, adoption numbers rose dramatically in response to the wartime illegitimate baby boom, and then stayed buoyant up to 1949 with more than 17,000 babies or children adopted per year. After that, numbers up to and including 1961 were an average of 12,635 per year, nearly double the figure for 1939. Twenty years after the Adoption Act came into being, the notion of adoption as a positive move was becoming firmly

established. However, there were times when babies and young children available for adoption were in short supply, and Margaret Kornitzer noted in the early 1950s that some adoption societies had waiting lists of several years for adoptive children.

In April 1951, there were 55 registered adoption societies in England and Wales, some localised and others more wide-ranging in their influence and activities. One of the new participants in the adoption scene was Dr Barnardo's, who in 1947 finally registered as an adoption society, much later than just about all the other organisations of its kind. The NCUMC had also come round to the idea of adoption in the 1950s, presumably their reluctance to adopt children was overcome by the general conviction that it was now the best thing to do for all concerned in some instances.

Mother and Baby Homes Post-1945

Mother and Baby Homes were still a popular – indeed, in many cases, inevitable – choice for pregnant single women, for a variety of reasons. They provided a place of safety if the woman's family had turned their backs on her; camaraderie with other women in the same position; some supervision of the pregnancy; discretion; and the opportunity to place the baby for adoption at the appropriate time. If the mother decided to keep the baby, some support with building a life with the baby may be offered too.

Other reasons for mothers agreeing to go into such a home included fear of the stigma their pregnancy would inflict on their families, and it gave them the opportunity for space away from their family in which to make a genuinely personal decision as to what to do after the baby's birth. They were, in a sense, 'cottage homes' for the women, although the accommodation came in a huge variety of shapes and sizes according to what buildings each organisation had been able to acquire, or had had donated to them.

Some homes were on the edge of town, where greater discretion could be assured, but others were surprisingly central to everyday life. One such Church of England Mother and Baby Home was in Chatham Street in Stockport, Greater Manchester. Chatham Street is in Edgeley, a very typical late-nineteenth-century suburb of Stockport, not that far from the town centre. Here, many streets of terraced houses are interspersed with slightly larger villas, of which this home is an example. It is a very

135

typical residence of its type built in about 1900: semi-detached, bay windows to the front, with no extensions or extras to accommodate more than what looks like the original three/four bedrooms – bearing in mind that the warden would have to have a room too. It has a brick-walled garden of sufficient size for hanging out washing and it is roughly half way along the middle of a long street – in one direction you can see the rooftop of the Town Hall, and in the other direction is a T-junction with a row of shops – these days, in need of refurbishment but no doubt 50 years ago they were useful local amenities.

Also, opposite the row of shops is the parish church, which is no doubt where the mothers went, as the home was run by the Church of England (which probably also explains its location). A little further away, about ten minutes' stroll – maybe more if you are heavily pregnant – is the high street for Edgeley with plenty of early twentieth-century-style shop buildings. Opposite the Town Hall was the Infirmary, which is where the girls would have had their babies – a very short taxi ride or car ride away.

What is intriguing about this home is how central it is – almost as if the mothers were being 'hidden in plain sight', right under everyone's noses. There is nothing out-of-town about it and given the very close proximity of the neighbours and the close-knit nature of such suburbs, all the nearby residents must have known what the house was being used for. It is a poignant experience even today walking up and down the street, wondering what it would be like for those mothers-to-be, watched and commented on by neighbours as they went for afternoon walks or to the shops for bits and pieces, then later on quietly arriving home with their baby. Other neighbours would have seen the terry napkins and baby clothes on the washing line; still more locals may have wondered about the 'respectable couples' going into the house to see, or collect a baby.

Another Mother and Baby Home in Vernon Street, Derby (originally in Gerard Street) strove to make the environment as homely and comfortable as possible. In 1950, Miss Brien, the temporary superintendent of the home, was campaigning for new or improved furniture and fittings. The home had recently had a second bathroom fitted, and had two large south-facing rooms for the girls, one a sitting room and the other a bedroom; a third room was reserved for new mothers just back from hospital. The nursery had a sink, gas ring and suitably decorated walls. The home was run by the Derby and Derbyshire

136

Association for the Help and Protection of Girls, and its role was to take in the mothers-to-be a month before confinement, and to allow them to stay on with their babies for a few weeks after the birth. Apart from any other help, the ethos was to allow the women to escape the stress, humiliation and pressure of their families and to mix with other mothers in the same position as themselves.

For mothers who wanted to keep their baby, they would assist in finding a job and put them in touch with other agencies who would help them. If the mother wished to put up her child for adoption, or place it in a children's home, they helped with that too. At the time of Miss Brien's incumbency the home was appealing for gardening tools, accessories such as mats, linoleum and mirrors, and a writing desk, plus comfortable chairs or help with re-upholstering the old ones. The home was trying hard to improve the environment for the mothers and their babies, and make it a place of refuge rather than punishment, and one can only hope that it succeeded.

A little later on, in the mid 1960s, the author Jill Nicholson undertook a survey of mother and baby homes on behalf of the National Council for the Unmarried Mother and her Child, and the results of her research make fascinating reading, if only because it reveals that in their basic form, nothing much had changed in these homes since the late 1950s. Ms Nicholson found that one in six of all extra marital pregnancies (up to 12,000 a year at the time of the study) were supported through these establishments, even though most of the residents had some contact with their own families – for example, two-thirds of the mothers had had some contact with their own mother after being admitted to the homes.

In addition, women in the north of England received a more sympathetic response from the local community than elsewhere, which would have helped the mothers at the Stockport home, for instance, in the closely built suburban streets of Edgeley. Some homes had their own maternity units, which saved the younger mothers from having to be alongside married women, and this shielded them from adverse comments from people in hospitals.

Most homes were provided by church bodies, but the residents did not feel on the whole that religion was 'pushed' on them, even though the author encountered some among the staff who regarded child-bearing outside marriage as a sin. However, many residents were expected to attend church and prayers which, for the non-religious, was at least an opportunity for a break from routine. One faith-based aspect of the homes that residents did find of help was the visits of a chaplain, as presumably it gave the opportunity for one-to-one conversations about the mother's situation. Most of the homes only took the mothers for about six weeks before and six weeks after the birth of the baby, so there was little time for the one-third of the mothers who would not be returning to their families to decide what to do and, even with the help of welfare workers, to arrange accommodation for herself and her new baby. The vast majority of the women were unmarried and were having their first baby, and they had jobs when the babies were conceived. Sadly, only just over a quarter of the putative fathers kept in touch with the mothers, and approximately another quarter did not know about the baby.

There does seem to have been friction within the homes – sometimes groups of residents would polarise and there would be tension between them, and sometimes it was between the residents and the staff, mainly the matron or manager. It is possible this was a simple but strong difference in the understanding of the *raison d'etre* of the home. Primarily of course, its priority had to be the welfare of the residents and their babies, and staff may have had strong views on how that could best be safeguarded. This could be seen as overbearing by some residents even though it was done 'for their own good'. The mothers were facing not only a life-changing event – the birth of their baby – but time spent learning to look after the baby, while for many, at the same time, they had to face the equally life-changing decision to give up their new baby, with all the distress that would entail.

Most residents were experiencing their first pregnancies, but it seems that some staff at the homes came across as overly controlling towards the care of the baby, rather than supportive. Some mothers merely wanted a place of safety in which to have their baby, and they resented being lectured about their sinful behaviour as happened in some homes. They certainly did not want to be subject to rules and regulations such as set visiting times, where or if they could smoke, and onerous levels of compulsory chores and housework (although most women were happy to do their fair share). There seems to have been confusion over the way the different adoption societies worked, and a lack of people to confide in – this was not an era that necessarily recognised the value of counselling.

In many homes, material conditions such as decorations and furniture had improved little since the 1950s. Often the mothers had to share rooms – most likely the case in the Edgeley home, for instance – and often the furniture, décor and overall ambience was dreary and dated. Privacy for personal hygiene, such as washes, and breastfeeding the baby, was at a premium, but to be fair, the accommodation for resident staff was no better.

As in Eleanor's story below, chores and housework were generally done in the morning, and afternoons and evenings were for free time or for doing craft, knitting and so on, although surprisingly none of this free time was used for mother and baby, or similar classes, and as a result, some of the mothers were woefully ignorant of what would happen when they went into labour. Apart from housework, the residents often helped to make the meals, which were generally adequate.

Once the baby had been born, mothers were not always given help with their mothering skills and complained that they did not have enough time to bond with their babies outside of feeding times; some homes did not permit women to take photographs of their soon-to-be-adopted babies. Some mothers complained of being patronised or over-criticised by welfare workers or the matron of the home.

However, one of the biggest advantages, it would seem, of these homes was the camaraderie that could develop between the mothers, which would have gone a long way to making up for the perceived inadequacies of the mother and baby homes. It should, in fairness, be pointed out that there were some excellent mother and baby homes with modern facilities, kindly and attentive staff and a liberal ambience.

Guiding the New Parents
The number of adoptions stabilised at about 13,000 per year in the 1950s, while in that decade the number of registered births outside marriage remained between 30,000 and 40,000, only rising sharply at the end of the 1950s.

Fundraising continued to be a vital source of raising cash for the adoption societies and it was something The Children's Society was particularly adept at. Plate 6 shows a postcard specially printed for the society to be used as a thank you note for a donation and posted in 1955. The group of happy, well nourished children fills the front of the postcard to remind the public how their money will be spent, but the children are not so well presented as to make the potential contributor think that the society had enough money to 'spoil' their young charges. A message from the secretary is printed on the reverse of the card: 'May I on behalf of our 5,000 children say "thank you" for your kind gift? Your sympathy and interest in our work is much appreciated and most encouraging in these difficult times' – this final comment no doubt being a reference to the post-war difficulties affecting Britain in the 1950s.

At the same time, as state intervention was helping all children and continuing to consolidate its role almost as a surrogate parent in many ways, so adoption almost became an 'industry', with well over fifty adoption agencies in operation at this time. Experts were writing and publishing at length about the process and its consequences, as well as penning helpful guides for prospective adoptive parents to support them through this life-changing journey.

Margaret Kornitzer was a highly respected expert on the subject and wrote many pieces of quality research and advice about adoption, but one of her best known was written for The Children's Society in about 1950. It was a booklet called *A Baby is Adopted* and the cover shows a photo of a typically cute, 'ideal' baby with obligatory quiff (see Plate 8), a baby who could happily have graced the pages of any of the popular women's magazines of the day. In the endorsement at the front of the booklet written by Dr Carruthers Corfield, Chairman of the Executive Committee, he enthuses about the 'moving history' which 'should be read by all those wishing to adopt a child and ... [*which would*] show would-be adopters the wisdom of enlisting the sympathy of a society whose aim is to take the very greatest care that the child is fit in every way for adoption'.

The booklet follows a fictional couple as they prepare to adopt a baby and in doing so, it shows the reader what has to be done and considered in the process. Once the rather cloying style of the narrative has been put aside, it contains some sound advice for prospective adoptive parents, but it also features a contrasting story about a young woman who circumvents all the legal adoption procedures and privately adopts a child she hears about through acquaintances. She wants a baby because she is lonely when her husband is out at work and because, she says, 'I suffer from my nerves.' She is portrayed as impulsive and indeed selfish; she has an 'interest in clothes and dancing', and is shown as wanting a child for her own ends and not for the purpose of loving the child for itself. It is an unmitigated disaster as the baby turns out to have a congenital problem and dies; she is not a child who at the time would have been put forward for adoption by an adoption society, had the correct route been taken.

There is also a gentle warning in the booklet about prejudice – the young woman who privately adopts the child tells her friend (the would-be legal adopter) that her baby is 'quite legitimate. I don't think I could bring myself to consider anything else, you know.' When challenged about the illegality of what she is doing, she retorts, 'If I'm not fit to adopt a child, I don't know who is.' The message is clear: anyone who will not be patient and follow the protocols of legal adoption; who wants a child for selfish or inappropriate reasons; or (and this is a relatively new development) holds a prejudice against illegitimate children as being somehow inferior to any other child, was not a suitable adoptive parent.

The stable married couple who do the right thing and adopt a baby legally and all above board, and are united in their desire to do this, do indeed take on an illegitimate child – however, the story does make it clear that the mother of the baby was a respectable girl who had made the one mistake, and was now hoping to marry a decent young man (not her baby's father) and make a fresh start.

However, the anxiety about public perceptions of adopted children is also reflected in the booklet – when the couple in the story finally get as far as the court hearing where their adoption of a baby is confirmed, the judge tells them about all the paperwork required, and also about the short birth certificate that can be issued for a baby. This was first used in 1947 and one of the reasons it was introduced was because of the revealing nature of the long adoptive certificate issued by the court, which broadcasts the adoption loud and clear. The short version enabled an adopted person to go through their life without having to reveal that they were adopted; however, it also enabled adoptive parents to conceal the fact that their child was adopted, even from the child themselves.

The Appendix at the rear of this book reproduces the Appendix provided in the booklet, which gives a detailed list of the procedures and responsibilities involved in adopting a child. All the expected issues are there: health concerns of both adopters and child; a reference to the mental health of the child (so that potential behavioural issues were raised early on in the process); a concern for the moral and spiritual welfare of the child with the insistence on married adopters and baptism; and a determination to legally oversee and complete the adoption so that the last door between birth and adoptive families is closed, often for good.

Adoptive parents could also now remain anonymous, if they so wished. It would seem that by the 1950s, there was a sense that adoption was becoming respectable and above board.

This rise in the respectability of adoption as a means of family construction brought added pressures on the would-be parents. They were expected to be paragons of parenthood in every way, and those who had 'failed' – other than in failing to conceive their own child – were viewed with suspicion. In 1949, the Western National Adoption Society (WNAS) confirmed that applications should be refused from would-be adoptive couples where one or both of them had been previously divorced – presumably the rationale was that such a failure in a relationship would make the couple more prone to leaving an adopted child in a precarious position – especially at a time when fewer women worked after marriage.

The Mayor of Bath commended the adoption society and their work in a speech at their annual meeting: 'I think you are doing a great deal, almost out of all proportion to your strength and support, to create the right conditions for the nation of tomorrow to grow up normal and balanced. For a child to have the right parents is a great thing, and I think that you do your best to see that the children have as ideal parents as your adoption system allows.'

In the following year when the most recent Adoption Act began to have an impact, one key change was the approval of a serial number rather than a name to identify the adopters, so that the birth mother and her family would not know their names. This meant that once the adoption was complete, the shutters had come down on the birth family and they had no way at all of finding out where the child was. However, as a safeguard for the birth mother, she could no longer consent to the adoption of her child until the baby was six weeks old.

The Act also allowed the mother of an illegitimate child to adopt her or him, but some courts took a less than enthusiastic approach to this, regarding it simply as a way to 'cover up' the illegitimate status of the child. As the NCUMC pointed out in a letter to *The Times* on 4 May 1957, all that mattered was the welfare of the child, and if that was best served by keeping birth mother and child together, then obstacles should not be placed in the way. The NCUMC was still helping thousands of unmarried mothers each year – in 1950/1 the figure was 5,675 new and ongoing cases, and at that time just after the war it was also acting as an agency forwarding money to the German babies of British soldiers.

The 1950 Act may have reinforced the notion of secrecy, but there was a body of opinion that adopted children should be told as soon as possible that they were not the natural children of their parents. In his speech to the Western National Adoption Society (WNAS) in 1949, the Mayor of Bath had supported this move, stating 'They should know the true position as soon as possible. To tell them when they reach maturity is a tremendous shock. Children should be advised; there is no reason to doubt that their affection will not continue.'

There is a contradiction here, as many adopted children, once told, have an intense curiosity about their birth family; one little girl adopted in the 1950s asked her adoptive mother over and over about how she came to be adopted, and never tired of hearing the story. She later went on to trace her birth mother after struggling for years with negative (and completely unfounded) feelings that she had been 'got rid of' because she was 'a naughty girl', even though her adoptive mother did not imply anything of the kind. Little wonder that some adoptive parents hid the truth despite the new advice to the contrary, feeling that it would cause instability in their much longed-for and carefully planned family.

Other interesting statistics emerged from the annual report of the WNAS in 1949. Over the previous year, 102 children had been placed in adoptive homes, of which so far, 79 were legalised. The society had had 328 enquiries offering a baby for adoption, but over half of these birth mothers did not formally come forward because they had changed their minds, had been refused as unsuitable, or had arranged a private adoption for their baby. Seemingly, despite the best efforts of the authorities, informal arrangements were still being made. The society therefore had more potential parents than it had babies, and had to temporarily close its waiting lists, asking applicants to wait for three months before applying for a boy, and six months for a girl.

The almost watertight exclusion of the birth family was to prove a growing issue as the decades progressed. As the number of adoptions increased, more studies were to show that children – even those adopted as babies – sometimes later developed an intense fascination for the birth family they had never known. In the absence of the facts, they might imagine a completely erroneous picture of the mystery family, especially the birth mother. One adopted person recalled:

I had an image in my head of a really rough family, that my mother had a brood of other children after me, and that I would have absolutely nothing in common with them and wouldn't want to know them. Looking back I can admit two things. One is that I was being a complete snob! And – how wrong I was. The family was the complete opposite of everything I had imagined.

It was not just expectations – a growing body of opinion was now theorising that to exclude birth relatives completely was not a good idea after all. This point of view had been present all along, but was now being taken much more seriously. Secrecy had been a priority with many of those involved in the early days of adoption, mainly for the benefit of the adoptive family, but also, they felt, for the child's welfare, to give the newly crafted family the opportunity to settle in together without fear of any 'interference' from the birth family.

However, at the same time as this secrecy was being encouraged, psychologists were putting forward the theory that such absolute separation was not in the best long-term interests of the child – especially someone adopted as a young child as opposed to a baby. Theorists such as John Bowlby (1951) researched the concept of attachment and concluded that babies and very young children attached to a single figure – such as a parent – and that this relationship acted as a prototype for all future social relationships. This relationship should be continuous for the first two years of life, and if this attachment was disrupted, it could have negative social, cognitive and emotional consequences. Bowlby referred to this disruption as 'maternal deprivation'. Some experts saw proof of this study in the intense grief some evacuated children suffered at the beginning of the 1939–45 war, but other still staunchly saw a move to a stable, comfortable home as all a child needed to re-establish their lives.

Whatever the ratio of opinion in the 1950s, Bowlby and his colleagues had provided some compelling food for thought and if nothing else, it would further encourage an adoptive family's determination to take a child as young as possible. It is therefore not surprising that in the 1950s, as in other decades, statistics reveal that the most popular choice of adoptive child was a baby, in that it was a blank canvas upon which the adoptive parents could paint their dream of a perfect child. Where the older child was concerned, there was a growing body of opinion that not only should the child be encouraged to talk about their adoption, but that the complete moratorium on the birth family was not constructive, and that at the very least, the child should be allowed to know something about their birth family and not just about the fact of adoption.

However, 3 per cent of adoption orders in the early 1950s were for children aged 15 years or older. A very small number of other children were born abroad – such as refugee children (although technically it was very difficult to adopt these), and another small percentage were children of colour. Of the children of colour, it was estimated in 1945 by the League of Coloured People (a British organisation working towards racial equality and equal civil rights) that approximately 550 of these children were allegedly the children of American soldiers of African-Caribbean or other non-Caucasian origins.

It was extremely difficult to find adoptive or foster parents for these children – this was an era of unbridled racial prejudice. As Margaret Kornitzer sadly commented in her 1952 book, 'The League of Coloured People is anxious to see more of these children adopted, particularly in the most urgent cases, which are made more urgent because so few high-grade foster mothers will take them.' Due to the low incomes of many people of colour living in Britain at that time, few could come forward to adopt a child, so most of the children of colour went to Caucasian adoptive families with all the cultural detachment that entailed.

Eleanor's Story
In Cheshire in the early months of 1954, Eleanor, a young woman in her twenties, found herself pregnant following a sexual assault. Her brother-in-law went to the culprit's house to confront him, but he had already fled. Eleanor also went there herself when she discovered she was pregnant, but was told he was still not there and was married anyway. It was clear that she would not be able to obtain any support from him.

The first problem she had to face was the sceptical response of her mother, who blamed her for 'encouraging' the assault. Abortion was still illegal, and would remain so until the 1960s, so that was not an option for her legally or morally. There was no choice but to go ahead with the pregnancy.

Although this was post-war Britain, the shining 'New Elizabethan' era of optimism and fresh beginnings after two world wars, in many ways life was the same as it had always been. In many families money was

145

desperately short and thousands of people were still living in substandard housing, and the moves towards a better society for all seemed to be dragging their heels. The same could be said about attitudes towards single mothers, as Eleanor was to find out.

She booked herself into the Church of England Mother and Baby Home near Nantwich and as the pregnancy progressed, gave up her clerical job and moved to south Cheshire. It was a long way from her home and family, as was the practice – single mothers-to-be were placed away from family for the sake of discretion for all concerned. This was particularly important if the pregnancy had been concealed, and the decision to have the baby adopted at birth had already been made, as it meant that the woman could return to her family and neighbourhood and start afresh as far as she was able.

The routine was common to many such establishments – the expectant mothers did chores in the morning, and then could rest or do their own thing in the afternoons. At first, Eleanor would walk into town every day in her free time, but before long the pregnancy began to take a toll on her. She was admitted to the Barony hospital six months into the pregnancy with pre-eclampsia, a condition dangerous to both mother and unborn baby, and had to submit to spending the rest of the pregnancy resting in bed. It was on admittance to hospital that she was stunned to learn following an x-ray that she was carrying twins. The next few months passed painfully slowly, but not without incident, as Eleanor recounts:

> *I had no visitors at all, no family and certainly not the biological father. The lady in the bed next to me had her husband visit regularly and they felt sorry for me because I had no-one – I had told them my husband was working away to explain why I was totally alone. Once the lady's husband brought me some flowers so I didn't feel so neglected. Then, one of the nurses told the lady that I was unmarried, and neither the lady nor her husband spoke to me again – they put me in coventry. I felt so humiliated and ashamed.*

What is telling about this anecdote is that not only the patient and her husband, but the nurse, thought badly of Eleanor because she was not married, and sadly this was not an isolated incident; many of the nursing staff behaved in a cold and offhand manner towards Eleanor because of her position.

The twins – a boy and a girl – were born at term but after a dangerously difficult labour, and while recuperating from the ordeal, Eleanor had choices to make. Giving up the children wasn't an option for her – she was determined to keep them and make a life for the three of them. She spent six weeks at the Mother and Baby Home recovering from an ordeal that nearly killed her and her babies, with around half a dozen other single mothers and the female welfare worker who looked after the home and the mothers. The manager of the home was unmarried, Eleanor was later to observe wryly, and had never had her own child. 'But she still used to boss us around and tell us what to do with our babies!'

At the end of this time, the twins went from the Mother and Baby Home into foster care until Eleanor could get back on her feet, find work, and establish a home she could take the babies back to. There followed a traumatic few years of desperately trying to do this, with the clandestine help of her older sister. At one point she found lodgings near her workplace, where she was settled for while. However, she then made the mistake of confiding in a work mate – a 'friend' – her story of the twins and her endeavours to build a life for the three of them.

The same day, on returning to her lodgings, she was confronted by the staunchly religious landlady and told she had to be out by the end of the week, as the landlady stated she ran a respectable house and did not want women like Eleanor in it. The so-called 'friend' from work had told the landlady Eleanor's secret. Meanwhile, Eleanor strived to maintain contact with her children, travelling long and convoluted journeys on public transport to see them whenever she could, building rare and precious memories of days out to North Wales and suffering the heartbreak of always having to say goodbye after each visit.

Finally, what looked like a ray of hope came along – Eleanor's married younger sister, who had young children of her own, offered to have the now toddler twins live with her, as she had just acquired her first home. At last, an end to visiting to the twins in the care of strangers seemed to be in sight – Eleanor's sister would take them in, while Eleanor built her life and found a suitable home for a fresh start. Unbelievably, tragedy struck again – Eleanor's sister collapsed and was admitted to hospital with meningococcal septicaemia and passed away, only weeks after she had taken in the twins. Eleanor moved into the house and looked after the twins and her sister's three sons for as long as she was able:

> *I took the twins to the shops in the morning, and in my hand I*
> *had a few pennies for our food. I would stand there looking at*
> *the coins and wondering how it could best be spent. Sometimes*
> *it would buy a quarter pound of minced beef, that was for the*
> *three of us. Usually I didn't eat and I lost so much weight, people*
> *said to me, 'Oh aren't you lovely and slim – how do you stay like*
> *that?' I didn't tell them I was like that because I had no food.*

Thoughts of the future began to haunt Eleanor. How would she clothe these growing children? What about shoes for the winter? The house had no hot water and was dilapidated and bleak. The safety net her sister had provided had been cruelly snatched away. This was not the life she had dreamed of building for her children. Solutions within the family did not seem workable to her, for a variety of reasons.

Almost at breaking point, Eleanor took the agonising decision to put her children up for adoption. As was sometimes the case, a couple offered to take one of the twins, but did not want both. They were turned down: 'They were to go together, or not at all,' Eleanor stated. Eventually, a childless couple came forward who seemed ideal. The husband had a steady job as an accounts clerk, and the wife had her own shop – highly respectable, a steady income, nice suburban home, and willing to take both children. The probationary period (see the Appendix) went well. Satisfied that this couple could give her twins a life that she could not provide, Eleanor signed the release papers.

After the adoption was complete and the adoption order issued, the children left the court with new surnames and new adoptive parents. One of the twins recalled the settling-in period:

> *We had lots of presents and fuss from the new family, it was*
> *overwhelming, in fact it was too much, and our new Mum liked*
> *to show us off. Once, we went to the regular wholesalers to get*
> *stock for the shop, and one of the staff said how like my new*
> *Mum I was. I think they said it to please her as they must have*
> *known we were adopted. I was nothing like her! I had strawberry*
> *blonde hair and her hair was jet black. But she went straight out*
> *and got her hair dyed the same colour as mine. She so wanted*
> *people to think we were her natural children.*

The twins only recalled one occasion when there was any follow-up contact with the adoption society:

> *I remember we had been adopted about six months and we were playing in the garden. Our adoptive Mum called us in to the kitchen where she was talking to a lady in a smart skirt suit, carrying a briefcase. The visitor asked us a few questions like 'Do you like living here?' and 'Are you happy?' and of course we said yes. Then Mum sent us back out to play. That was it! I don't remember any other follow-up for my brother and me. You didn't get any help as adoptive children in those days, and I needed it. I blamed myself for so many years for being the cause of the adoption and for putting my brother through that.*

In the meantime, Eleanor was suffering the terrible grief of a mother forced to say goodbye to her children for good. In the late 1950s, contact between birth and adoptive families was not allowed, so the parting was designed to be irrevocable. She faced the heartache of giving her daughter's toy pram to the local nursery. All the twins' papers and mementos had been sent with them to their new family, so she had nothing of that kind to treasure. She described the moment of parting as 'The most terrible moment of my life. I put my arms around them, and I said "Mummy loves you." Then they were gone.'

Eleanor was to see the twins one more time, however. A few months after the adoption, she accidentally saw her twins in a shopping area, hand-in-hand with their proud new adoptive mother. The shock was terrible; Eleanor desperately wanted to follow them, 'Just to look at them. But what was the point? I couldn't have them back. So I made myself walk away. It was horrible, horrible.' She did not see her children again for 54 years.

After she and the twins were reunited (Eleanor was traced by her daughter), she said:

> *I thought about my twins every birthday, Christmas, in fact every day we were apart. In the 1960s when the drug culture began, I worried because the twins were teenagers and I hoped they were not involved in anything like that. I thought about asking a*

149

famous TV show that granted wishes, to look for the twins, but I
was frightened they would blame me for having them adopted
and refuse to meet me. After they went, I was ill for a very long
time. Losing them nearly destroyed me.

This story illustrates numerous issues, some of which are typical of
many adoption-related stories, and some which are not. Eleanor had
applied to the courts for an affiliation order against the biological father
of her twins, and although it was granted, he was never traced. She does
not appear to have had any support in the form of financial advice
regarding help she may have been entitled to from the state. She faced
the humiliation of being regarded as a feckless and 'loose woman' by
some people in the community – even certain family members accused
her of having 'encouraged' the assault which resulted in the pregnancy,
which begs the question, how far had society's perceptions of the single
mother really advanced since the Victorian notion of the fallen woman?

Many charitable organisations would still only help the first-time
single mother, and marriage was still the ultimate goal for many women.
Post-adoption support for the adoptive family, both parents and children,
was often rudimentary at this time, and it would be years before this was
adequately addressed. As the 1960s approached, many single mothers
must have felt as marginalised as their counterparts were a century
before.

Changes on the Horizon: The 1960s and Beyond
However, by 1960, some attitudes were indeed starting to change. The
post-war baby boom children were growing up with very different ideas
and expectations to their parents and grandparents. Their baby care regime
had not been quite as rigid as it would have been in the interwar period
and post-war parents were sometimes more indulgent towards their
children than their own parents had been to them.

Never having known a lack of health care, and growing up with every
educational opportunity theoretically within their grasp in families with
more lenient parenting than before the war, they entered adult life with a
greater sense of optimism and modernism. A separate teenage culture –
which had started in the war with jive and the influence of Hollywood
style and slang – was developing, a development that accelerated as the
1960s approached. With its own music, lifestyle and mode of dress, this

teenage culture spawned new ways of thinking about social issues.

In 1958, Alan Sillitoe's gritty novel, *Saturday Night and Sunday Morning*, was published. It includes a grim description of a "gin and hot bath" induced abortion by one of the female characters, who is married with other children, but not willing to risk her husband finding out that the baby is not his. *The L Shaped Room*, published in 1960 by Lynne Reid Banks, focuses on a pregnant single woman who is turned out of the house by her judgemental father. The story is a sympathetic take on the young woman's plight, and it kept the profile of this put-upon group in the popular media. A film version released in 1962 was very popular but must, at the same time, have caused many young women to resolve never to allow themselves to end up in that position.

Stan Barstow's novel *A Kind of Loving* (also published in 1960) looked at a similar predicament from the father's point of view, although the man in this story is compelled to marry the mother of his baby. Barstow's and Sillitoe's novels – classic 'kitchen sink', that is, highly realistic, no holds barred stories – were filmed and brought the issue of unwanted pregnancies, back street and dangerous abortions and illicit sex right into the public eye. After the relative gentility of films in the late 1930s up to the 1950s, culture was changing dramatically. The Mental Deficiency Act of 1913 was repealed in 1959, taking away the ability of the authorities to commit women regarded as promiscuous or morally defective to a mental institution. If not at a local and family level, attitudes overall were showing signs of softening.

Throughout this period, back street abortions continued to wreak havoc on women's bodies, until the eventual passing of the 1967 Abortion Act which made abortion legal up to 28 weeks' gestation. The campaign to bring in abortion legislation was not one based on women's rights, but targeted more at the grievous public health problem caused by illegal abortion; no longer could a civilised society allow its women to be subjected to the butchery of the unscrupulous and unqualified.

In 1961, the NHS started to prescribe the contraceptive pill for married women only, at first. It is almost taken as a cultural given that 'The Pill' was a positive revolution for women, that it enabled them to take control of their own bodies, dictate when and with whom they had babies (if at all), and allow them to plan their childbearing around their other life plans – career, education, and so on. As the 1960s progressed, the pressure to release the pill to unmarried women grew and this was achieved in 1967. It was a remarkably reliable drug, which used extra hormones (synthetic oestrogen and progesterone) to prevent ovulation occurring and so stop conception.

The popular image of the mini-skirted swinger of the 1960s was still a dream to many girls in small provincial towns, but attitudes towards sex and sexuality were very slowly starting to change for everyone, should they choose to take advantage of it. By 1969, one million women – both married and unmarried – were taking the contraceptive pill.

Increasing numbers of girls went on to further and higher education and were able to take advantage of greater opportunities for advancement in the workplace; the campaigns for equality which women campaigners fought so hard for started to make a difference. Popular culture reflected the trend, although life remained difficult for the unmarried mothers who did become pregnant well into the 1970s. Eventually, the numbers of children born outside of marriage began to rise, while total numbers of live births registered fell in proportion. Middle-class couples began to reject marriage as an unnecessary or bourgeois concept, and as a result, what would have been regarded years before as illegitimate births were, by the 1980s, more often the children of stable partnerships who had simply not taken the step of getting married.

Demonization of the single mother – sometimes, the single father – became centred around the idea of the 'scrounger', someone who had illegitimate children in order to obtain financial security via state handouts and other benefits. A similar level of condemnation filled the newspapers and letters pages, not to mention certain political party conference speeches, but the rise and rise of the child born outside marriage became a permanent trend.

From 1961, the birth rate started to steadily fall while out of the total registrations of live births, the number of children born outside marriage rose. By 1990, 35 per cent of the 706,140 live births registered in England and Wales were babies born outside marriage, and that percentage has risen virtually every year since. Imagine the furore if that statistic had been released in Victorian Britain! At the same time, the numbers of children born either stabilised or declined and would have been immeasurably higher without the revolution in birth control of the later twentieth century.

Of these children born outside marriage, many more were in stable family homes or were with single parents who no longer felt the same pressure to give up their babies either to adoption, or to face life in an institution. As a result, the numbers of children adopted began to fall, but not until the mid 1970s – clearly the sexual revolution and the impact of the contraceptive pill took time to permeate the whole of society. Between 1974 and 1978, the number of adoption orders issued fell from 22,502 to 12,121, a dramatic reduction – ironically, the highest number up to this point was in 1968, at 24,831, right at the height of the 'Swinging Sixties' and a year after the contraceptive pill was made available to unmarried women. In 2011, the number of adoption orders totalled 4,777.

Society had changed beyond all recognition since the early days of adoption, but adoption as a concept – the notion that some children will always need a new family – remained a constant. There will also always be a need for the right people to take on the parenting role of children without families.

Postscript: Adoption as Quiet Revolution

Over the century of history charted within this narrative, adoption evolved from a dubious practice used to cover up the moral lapses of fallen women, to a reputable way of constructing one's family while at the same time giving a 'displaced' child the parental guidance, love and security she/he needs. Adoption became legally defined and much less amorphous in its nature than before, but the transfer of children from one parent figure to another has gone on for thousands of years.

Family historians tend to research their family histories in the hopes that the people they study are related to them. Given the choice of researching a biological great-grandmother or a step-great-grandmother – perhaps the second wife of their great-grandfather – the vast majority would research their female blood relative.

Yet how sure can we be that all the children in a family are definitely as they are stated on a census return, for instance? More than likely, we are already happily investigating the lives of some people who have no genetic link to us at all – the child who 'appears' on a census, seemingly from nowhere, and so on. Like it or not, 'chosen family' is a part of all our histories.

Throughout the centuries, adoption has been quietly effecting a revolution within the concept of family as it is seen in England and Wales. It proves that a family unit can transcend genetics and survive the experience, and was undoubtedly one of the factors which led to the loosening of the boundaries of what we see as family and a liberalisation of what constitutes family today. Adoption has always been the quiet revolution, and adopted children the unwitting, unknowing and quiet revolutionaries in family history.

Achieving legal adoption was not the revolution; it was merely the acknowledgement of a process that had been going on for millennia.

CHAPTER 6

Researching Adoption

Taking a Wider View

Whatever the reasons for an interest in adoption, it is useful to read around the topic by looking at the background history of childhood in this period. The books listed within the Recommended Reading list will prove invaluable, as will the list of recommended websites. The history of childhood can put family events into context and prevent the researcher feeling that events were unusual. It is impossible to take a balanced view of any historical trend or event unless it is put into context, and adoption is inextricably linked with topics like illegitimacy, social trends, legislative changes, the effects of war, and the growth of child welfare awareness.

First of All: Family Sources

This section is particularly aimed at those who wish to research an adoption within their family, whether their own or that of a relative. It should hardly need to be said that one should never research the adoption of a person from any perspective – birth or adoptive family – unless the full consent of those involved is obtained and pressure should never be brought to bear on anyone to give such consent.

One of the best sources of information about an adoption can be family members. When a child is adopted, undoubtedly gossip or at the very least comments will follow, among neighbours, relatives and family friends, and even if the adults of that generation are now gone, their children and grandchildren may have overheard information. Sometimes relatives will remember a flurry of interest and activity – presents being bought for the newcomer, and so on. One of Eleanor's twins (see Chapter 5), adopted at the age of three, recalled the many welcome presents given her and her twin brother when they became part of their new family. Other relatives may remember such times too, especially children whose natural curiosity over these stranger children would have made them alert to any mention of the new arrivals.

155

Adoptive parents may have confided the birth name of an adopted child to a relative or family friend, or given adoption papers to them for safe-keeping, so that the adopted child would not accidentally find them. If any records such as civil registration certificates are kept within the family, you can ask to see and possibly copy them, but of course, only with permission of the holder.

Photographs of the people concerned can be studied for clues – sometimes a potential adoptive parent would be sent a small photograph of the child they are being offered. This may have survived and may have useful background details of the child's original location, especially if they are scanned onto a computer and studied.

Look carefully at all the family archival resources you are offered, and pay particular attention to unusual addresses or letters from places not normally connected with known family; unidentified addresses in address books; photographs of children in unfamiliar or 'institutional' settings, etc.; old bank and savings books with regular payments being made into them which are not from family, and so on. They may prove to be blind alleys, but when it comes to adoption and illegitimacy, all possible sources of information should be followed up.

Adopted people may have memories of actually seeing adoption papers or correspondence relating to the adoption. One of Eleanor's twins went 'rooting' when she was eight years old, and discovered her birth surname when she found the twins' adoption papers in the family bureau. This was later invaluable in beginning the search for birth family and gave her many years to become accustomed to the notion of having a different name, and a different family out there somewhere. Some people come across such documents when clearing the homes of their adoptive parents when they pass away – that may even be the moment when they found out they were adopted. Of course, even in the era of adoption secrecy, some adoptive parents were completely open with their children and told them what they knew about the birth family.

Another word of caution must be noted here, as not all adoptive parents told their children the truth about the birth family. The twins were told many stories by their adoptive mother about their birth family and mother in particular, virtually all of which for whatever reason, proved to be completely without foundation. Sometimes adoptive parents, prompted by their own insecurities, will tell stories designed to deter children from seeking, rather than directly discouraging them or refusing information altogether. These stories could, over time, be transmitted down the generations as fact. Whatever you find out, it must be recorded carefully and in a logical manner so that you can use it to plan your next step.

Finally, as with all family history enquiries, you may reach a point where you have exhausted all avenues and not found the answers you seek. For instance, some single mothers have taken the identity of the father of their child to the grave with them, having revealed his identity to no one. This has to be accepted and respected, and the researcher must turn their attention to other queries. There is nothing else you can do.

Planning Your Research
Once you have exhausted all family sources (including friends of the family and neighbours if appropriate), you can decide what your next step will be. This may depend very much on what dates you are researching. Anything over a hundred years old is likely to be completely open access, so you should be able to go ahead and locate sources without worrying about how you are going to use it.

However, anything under a hundred years old, especially where it contains personal or sensitive details, will almost certainly be restricted. It may be possible to apply to the holder of the records to access them by invoking the Freedom of Information Act 2000. To find out about how to use this act, go to: *www.gov.uk/make-a-freedom-of-information-request/ the-freedom-of-information-act.*

If you are enquiring about information held by an organisation about you personally, you need to know about the Data Protection Act 1998. This Act controls how your personal information is used by organisations, businesses and the Government. Organisations are legally required to give you a copy of any information they have on you if you apply for it. There may be a charge for the search, and some sensitive records do have additional safeguards regarding their release.

The most straightforward way to approach any historical research is to make yourself a plan. Keep asking yourself questions – what do you want or need to know next? Have a focus for your enquiry. Enquiries to record repositories stating, 'I would like to know everything you have about ...' are less likely to be successful than those which are specific in their requirements.

Make a list of all these sources you would like to access and where you are likely to find them. If you are looking for details of an historic adoption over a hundred years old, there are numerous subscription-based websites that you can use. Browse each one carefully before you commit yourself to make sure you are getting the best set of records that you need for your own research.

Note: all records or record groups listed below are placed in alphabetical order for both pre and post 1926, and not in any implied order of relevance. The relevance of any group of records will depend upon the individual research project being undertaken.

Resources for Researching Adoption Before 1926
This list includes not only resources more directly connected with adoption or variations of adoption, but resources that refer to illegitimacy, child poverty and other issues mentioned in this book. Some sources will be relevant to more than one topic. Their relevance is noted in brackets after the title of the resource.

It is notoriously difficult to research adoptions which took place before the 1926 Adoption of Children Act, primarily because there are few formal records and the culture of secrecy surrounding it meant that few records were kept. Persistence is necessary, but avoid making huge 'leaps of faith' and making wild guesses.

A number of the sources given below can be found on a huge variety of free-to-access and subscription websites. If you decide to conduct your research through one website that you have to pay to use, take your time to browse the contents carefully. You may well find that record collections, for example, for a particular city such as Manchester, are split across more than one website, so consider purchasing credits if available, rather than paying out for a lengthy subscription.

Census Returns
(*Relevance:* adoption, fostering, institutions such as children's homes, orphanages and workhouses; family groups; indicators of social and economic status.)
Those currently available for the period 1851 to 1961 are: 1851, 1861, 1871, 1881, 1891, 1901 and 1911. The 1921 census will only be released in 2021, after one hundred years have elapsed. Because of assurances given to the population via the 1920 Census Act, it will not be released any earlier. The 1931 Census for England and Wales was completely

destroyed in a fire, and the 1941 Census was not taken because the country was at war. The 1881 Census is always available to view online free of charge, at least in transcribed format; sometimes you will have to pay to see digitised images of the census books.

The usual method employed to find a person listed on the census, is a search engine on a website. Most people use a full name to find a person, but it is possible to make searches on most sites by in-putting first/given names only, which is very useful if you do not know what surname an adopted or fostered child had been given. Add to this a date and place of birth and any other sound information you may have, but do not put in speculative information – sometimes the 'less is more' approach will give better results. Also, try searching for siblings, grandparents or extended family such as aunts or uncles, if finding the child alone is proving difficult. Use arrow buttons to browse the area around a family address, in case the child has been lodged nearby with neighbours, family friends, foster parents or extended family.

If you are looking for a child who was in an institution, it is useful to know that each institution, be it orphanage, workhouse or hospital, etc., was treated as a household in its own right. The entry will give the manager or head of the institution first, followed by their family if living in, staff, then the inmates. These may be in alphabetical order but this is not always the case, so scan the whole list if looking for siblings or parents. Be aware that as these inmates are not with family but in an impersonal environment. a less than accurate approach may have been taken by the person who filled in the census form with the spellings of names. This may also apply to ages and places of birth. Most of the institutions do not indicate the status of children, such as their legitimacy, but if a child has the same surname as the mother and she is recorded as single, she or he is most likely illegitimate.

The 'Fertility Census' included within the 1911 census return can be particularly useful, as it should show how many years a couple have been married, how many live births there have been within the marriage, and how many of their children were still living on the night of the census. Intriguing discrepancies can be spotted, with numbers of children clumsily altered and years of marriage changed to show all children born within marriage when the reality was different.

Location: without doubt, the best way nowadays to access the census returns is on the internet. All the major subscription websites have full coverage of the 1841 to 1911 census returns. However, *www.freecen.org.uk* is endeavouring to provide free-to-access coverage of the 1841, 1851, 1861, 1871 and 1891 census returns, but is not yet complete.

Change of Name Records

(***Relevance:*** adopted people, birth and adopted families who wished to formally change either their surname or their forename.)

There was, and still is, nothing to stop anyone calling themselves by whatever name they want, but for those who wanted to make it official, there were special procedures one could use. For those who adopted or took in a child before and even after 1926, it was easy to give the child a new surname and have them known by that at all times; hence the fact that 'displaced' children on census returns can sometimes have different names on different census returns.

For such informal changes, there are no official or permanent records other than the 'accidental' revelations in the usual family history resources. It is possible that a person who was taken in informally by a family as a child, would wish to officially change their name to that of their host family. Formal changes of surname may also be made by an adopted person who, perhaps, wished to revert to their birth name.

An official change of name was recorded in a Deed Poll and these are kept at the National Archives in Kew. The indexes or any other part of this collection are not available to view online. The records run from 1851 and it is possible to purchase a certified copy of the Deed Poll. From 1914, Deed Poll enrolments were announced in the *London Gazette*. To search this journal, consult: *www.thegazette.co.uk*.

However, if an extra fee was not paid to have the Deed Poll 'enrolled' in these records, they will not be in the index. The *Gazette* also published Change of Name Declarations which were necessary from 1939 to 1945, in order to prove your new identity so that National Registration records could be changed and a new registration card and ration book could be issued.

Church Registers

(***Relevance:*** illegitimate children, especially babies; marriages; extended family; birth father.)

Baptism Registers in the Anglican Church from the sixteenth century onwards show clear indications of the legitimacy or otherwise of a baby being baptised. Where there was a possibility of obtaining some form of maintenance payment from the biological father (or the man stated to be the father – it was difficult to prove one way or the other), the name of the father may be stated on the baptism entry. Otherwise, the name of the mother only and the child's name would be stated, an excellent indication, along with the mother and baby's surnames being the same, that the child is illegitimate. Up to 1837 and the advent of civil registration of life events, the father in the case of a married couple was all important as the entry was proof of paternity for the purposes of inheritance, so his absence speaks volumes.

After this date, both baptism and birth entries can be consulted in a search for a father's name.

Marriage Registers: These can be checked to see if the mother of an illegitimate child later married the father, or if she had parted with the child, went on to marry someone else (therefore acquiring a new married name).

Burial Registers: Only babies and young children tend to be listed by their illegitimate status in burial registers, which rarely give any details other than name and date of burial, especially before changes were made to the recording of burials under Rose's Act, which was passed in 1812.

Location: Local Archives or Diocesan Archives (often on the same site and administered by the secular county archive staff). Large numbers of parish and nonconformist registers are now being uploaded to the internet, mostly on subscription websites such as Ancestry and Findmypast. Check coverage on these websites to see if they have what you need.

Parish registers are also available on CD. It is rare for a place of worship to still hold its historic registers, but a minority do, especially if it is still in use (one parish church in Mid Wales is still using a burial register that holds entries dating from the 1850s and even earlier), or they may have facsimile copies which can be viewed. However, it easier to start online with your enquiry where you can.

Civil Registration

(***Relevance:*** illegitimate children; single mothers; infant mortality; maternal mortality; marriage of birth parent/s.)

From 1 July 1837, the civil (i.e., state, not church-run) registration of life events began. Since then, every birth, marriage or death occurring in England and Wales should have been registered. Despite a few teething problems, they mostly were and it is possible to purchase a certified copy of an entry, if you have the correct details to hand.

Problems will arise where a child's name has been changed since registration (most likely in pre 1926 private adoptions), but equally there are restrictions on who, apart from the adopted person themselves, can access them. The following records are available:

Birth Certificates: the section for birth father's details will usually be blank for an illegitimate child. Sometimes the middle name of a child will seem to indicate a family surname other than the mother's – possibly the father – but this must be corroborated from other sources. Be aware that if an illegitimate child prior to 1875 has a father named on the birth certificate, there were no restrictions up to this date for the mother to put any man down as the father. This of course had to be changed because of the obvious turmoil and false accusations it could and did cause.

Marriage Certificates: in the pre 1926 period, it is quite possible for a person who had been adopted, and knew their birth name, to revert back to it at the time of their marriage. This is not uncommon, and seems to represent for some a statement of their individuality and new autonomy as an adult. Occasionally, an illegitimate person will name a father on their marriage certificate, but this must to checked very carefully as it could be instead a close relative or 'adoptive' father. Check the names of the witnesses also, as they are usually close relatives, parents or friends of the family.

Location: Local Register Offices for direct application; the General Register Office for all applications for England and Wales. You cannot consult records at the General Register Office. The indexes are widely available online and you are expected to use them to find the details you need to make an application. Go to *www.gro.gov.uk* to browse their services and how to use them.

Institutions

(*Relevance:* illegitimacy; medical records; mental health; single mothers, adoption, fostering; orphanages and other children's homes; mother and baby homes; hospitals; County Asylums and mental hospitals; Cottage Homes; refuges.)

Many of these institutions were privately owned and run, short-lived, or kept chaotic or incomplete records, and the further back you go, the less likely they are generally to be efficient and extant. These records may be subject to restricted access, as they contain sensitive and personal details about individuals. Contact the relevant archive to ascertain what records have survived, what you may access, and how. You will need to be aware of sensitivities also, as some institutions have been the subject of allegations of ill-treatment of their charges. See also Poor Relief, below.

Records of institutions may include admissions registers, correspondence, medical histories, photographs, case notes, adoption records, accounts, publicity literature, news cuttings and photographs.

Location: for public institutions and some privately run organisations, contact the relevant local archives. However, many children's homes or orphanages run by independent organisations, such as religious orders, may have kept their own archive, in which case you will need to do some research on the location of the organisation's head office and approach the organisation direct. Some of the larger charities have their own dedicated staffed archive, in which case you would approach them direct.

Newspapers

(*Relevance:* reports of child trafficking, baby farming, child-centred charities and campaigning groups, institutions, mother and baby homes, adoption societies, advertisements for babies either to be adopted or looking for a child, contemporary opinions on all issues relating to the subject, parliamentary debates and details of Acts of Parliament, editorials about any aspect of the subject.)

All archives and record offices which specialise in a specific catchment area, such as an historic county boundary, will have a good selection of local newspapers with excellent coverage. However, unless you have a specific article or date in mind, it is not practical for the staff at an archive to undertake extensive searches for you, or if they are willing, you may have to pay a search fee. Many archives have a searchable online catalogue you can browse to obtain a list of what is available, which you can then use as a guide when looking at the growing number of websites where digitised and searchable newspapers are available to view and often to download.

The website *www.britishnewspaperarchive.co.uk* has an excellent selection of provincial newspapers and contains many references to the issues discussed in this book. At present the newspapers available cover the dates 1710-1959, but the website is regularly updated with more additions. It is possible to search the website free of charge and view the basic results, but a subscription is required to access the articles.

Other websites which include some newspapers as part of their portfolio of resources are: *www.ancestry.co.uk* and *www.findmypast.co.uk*. For national newspapers, The Times Digital Archive 1785–2006 and the Guardian and Observer Digital Archive 1791–2003 offer the best range of articles from national newspapers. These two archives are often provided free of charge to members of local public libraries as part of their online resources; check with your local library to see if they provide this service. For Wales, *http://welshnewspapers.llgc.org.uk/en/home* has the best online selection of newspapers for this nation, and includes Welsh language newspapers.

Location: for hard copy or microfilm of provincial newspapers, the relevant local archive. For all national newspapers, the British Library has a complete collection. The National Library of Wales – *www.llgc.org.uk* – has an excellent collection of Welsh newspapers in Welsh or English, also see details of the website above, which is being added to on a regular basis. Otherwise, websites as above.

Poor Law (see also Workhouse, below)
(*Relevance:* illegitimate children; single mothers; references to biological fathers; maintenance; living standards of paupers; treatment of single mothers and illegitimate children; boarding out/fostering of pauper children; workhouses.)
For the period 1850 to 1948 (when the Poor Laws were finally repealed with the advent of the National Health Service and new social service system), most records of interest will be held at the relevant local record

offices. These records may include maintenance orders in connection with the 1845 Bastardy Act, settlement and removal examinations and orders (unlikely to be found after 1900), general correspondence, correspondence regarding the adopting or boarding out of children in the control of the Guardians, and paperwork in connection with boarded out children. There may also be some payments of relief to women with very young families on an out-relief basis, that is, they remained in their own accomodation rather than going into the workhouse.

Settlement and Removal Papers
(*Relevance:* single mothers, illegitimate children, removal of pregnant women, pauper children, orphans, absconding fathers.)
A legal procedure by which individuals (almost always those claiming poor relief) could be compulsorily removed from a parish to a designated home parish or parish of legal settlement, this parish having a legal obligation to maintain the pauper. Removals were still taking place in the mid-nineteenth century, but the numbers of cases had diminished considerably. May include details of other family members, names of children, and lists of the parishes the person or family group have resided in.

Location: local archives. These records are not widely available online at the present time.

Vaccination Records
(*Relevance:* illegitimacy; name of mother; address.)
Vaccination of all babies against smallpox was compulsory from 1853 and registers were kept by the local registrar of the progress of the vaccinations. Illegitimate children stand out as having the same name as the mother, but no father's name recorded. Useful for confirmation of address and can stand as a reasonable substitute for a missing index entry in the civil registers.

Location: local archives. These records are not widely available online at the present time.

Workhouse Records
(*Relevance:* paupers, illegitimate children, deserted children, foundlings, single parents.)

Workhouses were often used as a safety net by single mothers and their children. The contact may begin when a woman gives birth in the workhouse (perhaps if her family refused to allow her to be at home for the lying in) and may continue until the child or children are older. Sometimes a woman may leave her children in the workhouse while she goes out to work or to look for work.

It is useful to remember that people did not necessarily languish continuously in the workhouse for years on end, but would take advantage of it when hard up or out of work (or possibly deserted by a partner/abandoned by family), so never assume that the one occasion you find them in there was not repeated – check a wider span of dates to be sure. You may find mother and child listed as inmates in a workhouse on the census returns (see also comments on the census, above), where the workhouse will be listed as one complete "household".

Other surviving records may include:

- Admissions books (which will give details such as age, parish of origin, and occupation for an adult, with less detail for a child)
- Discharge books
- records of births and deaths which occurred in the workhouse (after 1837, copies of birth and death certificates can be obtained from the General Register Office in the absence of birth and death records for the workhouse)
- local newspapers (for general stories and background)
- visual resources – photographs, plans, maps and sketches (for impressions of the buildings and facilities)

Location: Originals are usually housed at the local archives or county record office. You may find that the workhouse records, general poor relief records, and vaccination records are kept together. Some workhouse records are now available online via subscription websites such as *www.findmypast.co.uk*, and much general information of note can be found on Peter Higginbotham's excellent website *www.workhouses. org.uk*. This website is free to access. The survival rates of workhouse records can be very variable, always check before planning a visit to the records office.

Resources for Researching Adoption After 1926

For those who wish to research adoptions from the very recent past, such as their own, one of the most important factors to remember, especially where one or more of the key individuals involved is still alive, is to be aware of the sensitivities of the situation. There are, of course, some adopted people who have no feelings on the subject either way – or they may not think they do, until the subject is raised. Other people are very sensitive about the subject and may need additional support if they are to explore the issues raised by their own, or their child's, adoption. If you are in any doubt as to how to begin this search, or you are an adopted person who wishes to make contact with your birth relatives, you are strongly urged to contact the relevant authorities listed below.

Another word of caution, especially if you are researching the adoption of a close family relative or your own adoption: once you have found out the facts, you can never 'un-know' them; they are with you forever. Think carefully before you proceed. Are you as prepared as you can be for all eventualities, both factual and emotional? Do you have support from family, professionals and agencies as appropriate? (All those adopted before 1975 must have compulsory counselling before they access their records, in any case.) This may not apply to adoptions before living memory, but finding out about later adoptions if those involved are still living, can be life-changing.

Take your time, take one step at a time, and if at any point in the process you need to pause or stop completely, do so. Never lose control of the search, especially if you are the adopted person or birth parent. Do not be pressurised by other people into starting or continuing the search. Be kind to yourself at all times.

Undoubtedly, one of the key websites for anyone requiring basic information about institutions, organisations and people connected with adoption in the twentieth century, is *www.adoptionsearchreunion.org.uk*. It offers comprehensive information about locating adoption records, looking for information about mother and baby homes, your rights regarding contact, and much more relating to adoptions up to 30 December 2005. This is an active website which is often updated, so check back regularly if you are searching for information. It also offers advice and support for those who are planning to make contact with birth or adoptive relatives, and also offers advice for those who do not wish to have contact – bearing in mind, of course, that no one is obliged to have contact with anyone should they not wish to.

The website also has a superb page giving advice on using social networking websites for your research and in particular for making contact with birth or adoptive relatives: *www.adoptionsearchreunion. org.uk/contact/socialnetworking* and you are strongly urged to read this before you use such websites as part of your research, whether it is purely adoption-related or of a wider, family history nature.

Change of Name Records
(See the entry for this subject in the pre 1926 resources, above.)

Church Records
Most of the comments for the church records from the previous section apply here. In addition, the 1958 Adoption Act changed the wording of the baptism entry of an adopted child to show 'Adopted son or daughter of ...' whereas previously adoptive parents had asked for their child to be recorded as their natural child. This applies to the registers of the Church of England.

Civil Registration
(*Relevance:* details of birth family/parent, addresses, death details, adoption details.)

Adoption Certificates: the Adoptions Section of the General Register Office is based at their headquarters in Southport, Lancashire. Any legally adopted person over the age of 18 may have access to their birth records, and order a copy of their original birth certificate from this centre (births in England and Wales only).

Obviously, to order a certificate you must have some details of your birth identity; if you do not, you may apply to find out what records there are. The web page *www.gov.uk/adoption-records* has downloadable forms you can use to apply for access to birth records for England and Wales and also gives the address of the Adoptions Section of the General Register Office in Southport.

The General Register Office also holds the Adoption Contact Register. You can apply to have your name and contact details put on this if you are searching for contact with the adoptive or birth family;

alternatively, you can add your name if you do *not* wish to have any contact. If other relatives have added their names to the list or do so in the future, you will be informed of this if they are seeking contact.

As a word of encouragement, just because relatives have not added their names to the contact register does not mean they are not interested or receptive to the idea of contact – they may not be aware the register exists. Therefore, do not be too downhearted if your relatives are not there. However, as always, proceed with caution and utilise all professional help as appropriate.

You cannot view any adoption indexes or registers online, for obvious reasons of confidentiality.

Short Birth Certificates: these were introduced to conceal the fact of the adoption and ensure discretion for the adoptive child and their family, but they do reveal the adoption in subtle ways. It will have been issued by the Registrar General, not a local Superintendant Registrar, and instead of the normal volume and page number (or National Health Service Number after 1939), it will have the serial number for the relevant entry in the Adopted Children Register.

A full, adoptive birth certificate was issued by the Registrar General after the court proceedings and shows the following: the date and court of the order, the child's new adoptive forename/s and surname which was legal from the date of the order, the gender of the child, and the name, surname, occupations and address of the adoptive parents. If issued after 1950, it will also show country of birth.

If you are the adopted person and do not know anything about your background, you may apply to see your original birth entry. If you were adopted before 12 November 1975, you must have compulsory counselling to ascertain if you are able to proceed with the request. If you know your original birth details there is nothing to stop you sending for your original birth certificate like any other.

Marriage Certificates: Unless the adopted person has formally changed their name from that on the adoption paperwork, their name on a marriage certificate will be their adoptive name/s.

Birth Certificates other than adoptive: Where an adopted person has had children, their names as parents will most likely be recorded as their adopted names unless they made a conscious decision to reclaim and use their birth name.

Electoral Registers
(***Relevance:*** locations of individuals; lists of voters at a given address.)
Electoral Registers are available in any local authority and more than likely in large local libraries and archives. There are commercial websites which provide searchable databases of the registers, such as *www.192.com*, but they can be expensive to use. Bear in mind that individuals can request to remain private and you may not find them on the registers as a result.

Medical Records
(***Relevance:*** personal details, possible references to adoption, fostering, birth family details.)
Sometimes, the personal records of an adopted person contain hints as to the adoption and its background. One young man adopted in the 1950s sneaked a look at his GP notes when his doctor stepped out of the room for a moment and saw a list of his foster homes and other notes, including the reason he had been adopted in the first place.

Under the 1998 Data Protection Act, you have a right to access any records kept by the NHS about you. You can apply to your GP, a hospital if it is known, and patient services manager, making what is known as a 'Subject Access Request'. Try to give the provider as accurate an idea of the dates of the events you are asking about to help them with their search, especially if you are trying to access hospital records. The provider will then consider your request and let you know if they have approved it. You should receive a response in approximately three weeks. Be aware that everyone's personal medical records will be different and you are not guaranteed to find the answers to your questions even if you go ahead with such a request.

Should you wish to access the records of a deceased person, bear in mind that GP records are destroyed after ten years. Also, under the Access to Health Records Act 1990, you may only access these records if you are a personal representative, an executor, or someone who has a claim resulting from the death (who could be a relative or another person). Contact the deceased person's GP to find out where the records have been transferred to in order to proceed with the application. You may have to pay a fee for this service.

National Registration of 1939
(*Relevance:* confirmation of whereabouts/addresses; people at one address; names; marital status, occupation.)
The National Registration of 1939 was based on the general structure of what would have been the 1941 census return, and is often referred to as a quasi census because of this. However, it is very expensive to access (£42 per enquiry at the time of writing, which is non-refundable even if the search is unsuccessful), and restricting in what it gives by way of information. It could, however, be useful to find out the whereabouts of evacuated people of all ages. Only information about persons who are now deceased will be released.

Location: These records are held by the Health and Social Care Information Centre in Southport. They are not available for the public to view, or browse, in person, only postal applications will be accepted. For a summary and to find out how to access information, go to *www.hscic.gov.uk/register-service*. However, *www.findmypast.co.uk* are in the process of digitising these records and at the time of writing, plan to have them available online by approximately 2015/16. For updates on this project, you can register an interest here: *www.1939register.co.uk*.

Newspapers
In the case of newspapers, all comments in the pre-1926 selection of sources apply to post 1926 newspapers. However, there may be more local newspapers available in the twentieth century, with more photographs. The local archive will be able to advise.

Other Sources

Evacuees: In recent years there has been keen interest in the lives of children who were evacuated at the beginning of World War Two. There are plenty of websites with informative autobiographical accounts, general social history books and many evocative visual resources. These would be a good place to start research on this subject, especially local histories if the destination of an evacuated child is known.

Local archives may have records relating to evacuation, but the quantity, quality and survival rates will vary greatly. Some will refer to children by name and others do not. Not all records will be available for inspection.

A search on the website using the key word 'evacuees' *www.national archives.gov.uk/a2a* will give you a list of archives which could have records of interest. These may include:

- Requisition documents relating to properties to be used as billets
- School records: school log books, and admissions registers
- Lists/registers of evacuees which may include names, ages, general comments, where from, sometimes includes identities of mothers evacuated with their babies or very young children
- Lists of billets and the householders, sometimes with names of children placed there
- Lists of equipment available for loan to householders with evacuees, such as beds and bedding, cots, kitchen equipment, chairs, and so on
- Lists of children, teachers and helpers from one particular destination
- Newspaper cuttings
- Accounts books
- Personal papers such as letters
- Autobiographical accounts
- Video and audio sources such as oral history interviews, home movie footage and newsreel footage
- Official papers such as Home Office circulars
- WVS (Women's Voluntary Service) papers such as minute books giving details of billets, etc.
- Hospital and other medical and sick bay records.

Be aware that some records, such as those for schools and hospitals, and lists of evacuees giving personal details, may be closed for reasons of privacy. Contact the relevant archive for more details.

Kindertransport Children: Most of the records for the children who came over on the Kindertransport are maintained by World Jewish Relief, the organisation which played a substantial role in bringing the children to Great Britain. Copies of the records for individual 'kind' can be supplied to family members on the payment of a small fee to cover administrative costs, and on production of authorised documentation. They are based at Oscar Joseph House, 54 Crewys Road, London, NW2 2AD. Tel. 020 8736 1250. Website: *www.wjr.org.uk.*

Mass Observation: This has been placed in 'other' records as it did not generate records specific to adoption, but does provide a fascinating background to people's thoughts and opinions during its heyday from 1937 to 1950. However, the project continues and has regular 'Mass Observation Days' where the public can submit a diary for a specified day to the archive. The diaries, reports and other documents it generated are now archived at the University of Sussex in their Special Collections section. You can visit the archive and do research on it in person.

You can explore the 'Mass Obs', as it is affectionately known, at: *www.massobs.org.uk.* Also, many of the earlier diaries have been digitised and put online at: *www.massobservation.amdigital.co.uk/index.aspx* and can be searched for specific topics or key words. You will need a subscription to access this latter website.

New Regulations – November 2014
New Government rules due to come into force by November 2014 will enable all relatives of adopted adults, such as children and grandchildren, to find out about their birth family, with particular reference to inherited medical conditions. They will also assist with contacting birth family through intermediary services. However, safeguards will also be in place to protect the private family life of adopted people and the adopted person's consent must be obtained before contact or the sharing of information is facilitated. The relevant press release can be consulted here: https://www.gov.uk/government/ news/relatives-of-adopted-adults-now-able-to-trace-family-tree. Only time will tell what the impact of this change will be, how easy it will be to access the birth family information, and how wide ranging that information can be. Researchers from both birth and adoptive families are strongly advised to make extensive enquiries about the new rules before going forward, so that they fully understand the implications for themselves and others.

Appendix

Adoption Procedure: Taken from the Booklet, *A Baby is Adopted*, by Margaret Kornitzer and published by The Children's Society (1950)

1. APPLICATION TO ADOPTION SOCIETY
    A. Applicants must be:-
        (i)   Practising members of the Church of England
        (ii)   Domiciled in England and Wales
        (iii) One over 25 and both under 46 years of age
    B. Applicants must furnish:
        (i)   Medical certificate regarding sterility
        (ii)   Copy of marriage certificate
        (iii) Completed application form – references will be taken up by the society. A visit will be made by the Society's Welfare Officer and possibly Visitor on behalf of the Children's Officer

2. CONSIDERATION OF APPLICATION BY SOCIETY'S ADOPTION COMMITTEE
    Approval and entry of name on waiting list

3. INTRODUCTION TO CHILD
    (a) History and medical reports sent for consideration of adopters
    (b) Visit to nursery

4. PROBATIONARY PERIOD OF AT LEAST THREE MONTHS
    (a) Local Authority, i.e. Children's Officer to be notified by the prospective adopters immediately child is in their care of their intention in due course to apply for an Adoption Order in respect of the infant. Probationary period commences from date of notification.
    (b) During probationary period visits may be expected from the Society's Welfare Officer and representative of the Children's

Officer. If child is under five years of age the Local Authority Health Visitor will also call.

(c) Application to Court, Juvenile or County for Consent Forms and Application Forms. If identity to be kept secret, Serial Number must be applied for.

When application is lodged in court, documents required are:

(i) Full copy of child's Birth Certificate

(ii) A medical certificate as to the child's physical and mental health

(iii) Adopters' Marriage Certificate

(iv) Consent Form(s) signed by parent(s) or guardian

Child's name can be changed or added to and the application to the Court makes provision for this.

After receiving completed application the Court will appoint a 'guardian *ad litem*' for the child, whose duty it is to enquire fully into all the circumstances and report thereon when the case is heard.

5. EFFECT OF AN ADOPTION ORDER

(a) After an Adoption Order has been made, all rights and duties of adopters will be those of natural parents, and in the event of adopters making a Will after the date of the Adoption Order or of dying, intestate, the adopted child will be treated as the adopter's own child. It is essential in the case of a Will made before the adoption to make a new Will, or add a codicil to the old one, if the adopters wish the adopted child to participate in their estate.

(b) Child must be registered in his or her new names at the Food Office, School, Post Office Savings Bank, etc.

6. CORRECTED BIRTH CERTIFICATE

When an Adoption Order has been made the Court will notify the Registrar-General of the fact. After the adoption is registered, the adopters will be notified by the Registrar-General and they can then obtain a copy of the Adoption Certificate, which takes the place of the original Birth Certificate.

Two types of certificate are available:-
(i) A full reproduction of the entry in the Adopted Children Register (fee 2/6*d*).
(ii) A shortened certificate which bears no reference to adoption and shows only the child's new names, sex, date and place of birth (fee 6*d*).

7. BAPTISM
It is normally desirable to wait until the Adoption Order has been granted before arranging for this to be done so that the names by which the child will in future be known appear in the register and on the baptismal certificate. (If baptism is administered during the probationary period it will be necessary for the child's present names (and surname) to be used and they will be entered in the baptismal register.) If the child has been baptised before being placed with the adopters, there can be no second ceremony, but the clergy are generally willing to conduct a simple service of Blessing, whereby the child is received into the Church in his or her new name.

A 'Service of Blessing of an Adoption' has been prepared and further details can be obtained from the Society.

Further Reading

This is a comprehensive list of sources used by the author to research this topic.

Archival and Primary Sources
The following is a list of historical resources consulted during the research for this book. It can be used in conjunction with the research guide to obtain and use records to help with researching adoption, the history of childhood, and general social history for the period 1851 to 1961

Adoption Arrangements pre-1926
Correspondence regarding the adoption of Cassie Davies. Source: Conwy Archives

Census Enumerator's Returns and Related Papers
Census Enumerator's Returns, 1841, 1851, 1861, 1871, 1881, 1891, 1901, and 1911 for England and Wales

Census of Great Britain 1801–1851, Population Tables Volumes I and II (published 1852)

Originals are housed at the National Archives; however, they are also available in other formats and online – see the general research section for more information

Civil Registration
Copies of birth, marriage and death certificates (various) obtained from the General Register Office, Southport and various Local Register Offices

Crime and Petty Crime
The Stockport Town Thieves Book (register of petty criminals 1879 to 1938). Source: Cheshire Archives

Evacuation Records
Index to helpers 1941 onwards, Llandudno, Caernarfonshire
List of items loaned to fosterers in Llandudno, Caernarfonshire, 1939–45
Householders with blankets on loan, 1939–45, Llandudno, Caernarfonshire.
Source: Conwy Archives

Journals and Magazines
British Journal of Nursing, and Supplement
British Medical Journal
Englishwoman's Domestic Journal
Englishwoman's Review
Fortnightly Review
Freeman's Journal
Home Chat
Lady's Companion
Lady's Monthly Museum
Review of Reviews
Woman's Signal

Maintenance Arrangements
Private arrangements for the maintenance of illegitimate children, various, to 1913. Source: Conwy Archives, Llandudno

Mass Observation Archive
This is now housed within the University of Sussex Special Collections at:
The Keep,
Woollards Way,
Brighton,
BN1 9BP

Alternatively, a wide selection of extracts from the collection can be found at www.massobservation.amdigital.co.uk/Index.aspx

Newspapers
Aberdeen Daily Journal
Bath Chronicle and weekly Gazette

FURTHER READING

Belfast News-Letter
Brisbane Courier
Cambrian Daily Leader
Chelmsford Chronicle
Chronicle
Daily Mail
Derby Daily Telegraph
Derby Evening Telegraph
Edinburgh Evening News
Essex County Chronicle
Evening Telegraph
Evening Telegraph and Star
Exeter and Plymouth Gazette
Gloucester Citizen
Hull Daily Mail
Hull Packet and East Riding Times
Illustrated Usk Observer and Raglan Herald
Leicester Chronicle
Liverpool Mercury
Manchester Courier and Lancashire General Advertiser
Manchester Evening News
Manchester Mercury
Merthyr Telegraph and General Advertiser
Monmouthshire Merlin
New Zealand Herald
Pall Mall Gazette
Portsmouth Evening News
Royal Cornwall Gazette
Sheffield Daily Telegraph
Tamworth Herald
Taunton Courier and Western Advertiser
The Times
Weekly Mail
Western Daily Press
Western Morning News
Western Times
York Herald
Yorkshire Evening Post

Parish Registers
Marriage registers for Haslingden, Lancashire. Available at the County Record Office for Lancashire, Preston

Parliamentary Papers
Acts of Parliament in date order:
1834 Poor Law Amendment Act
1844 Poor Law Amendment Act
1861 Offences Against the Person Act
1868 Poor Law Amendment Act
1872 Infant Life Protection Act
1872 Bastardy Laws Amendment Act
1874 Births and Deaths Registration Act
1886 Guardianship of Infants Act
1889 Poor Law Act
1889 Prevention of Cruelty to, and Protection of Children Act
1891 Custody of Children Act
1897 Infant Life Protection Act
1899 Poor Law Act
1908 Children Act
1911 National Insurance Act
1913 Mental Deficiency Act
1926 Adoption of Children Act
1926 Legitimacy Act
1930 Poor Law Act
1939 Adoption of Children (Regulation) Act (came into full operation 1943)
1945 Family Allowances Act
1948 Childrens Act
1948 National Assistance Act
1950 Adoption Act
1958 Adoption Act
1967 Abortion Act

Parliamentary Publications
Report from His Majesty's Commissioners for Inquiring into the Administration and Practical Operation of the Poor Laws, 1834
Report of the Committee on Child Adoption, 1921

Child Adoption Committee, First, Second and Third Reports, 1924–5, 1924–5, 1926
Report of the Departmental Committee on Adoption Societies and Agencies, 1936–7

Oral Histories

Please note that all of the private individuals who have shared their stories with the author in the course of researching this book have been given a commitment that their personal details will not be made public. All names have been changed, where a name has been used.

For sources of oral history accounts covering all aspects of life, The Oral History Collection at the British Library may prove useful. See www.bl.uk/oralhistory.

For other sound archives, including the North West Sound Archive, see: www.nwsoundarchive.co.uk and the National Screen and Sound Archive of Wales: www.archif.com

Quarter Sessions Records

Assorted Summons, presentments and other papers held at Cornwall Archives, Truro

Reference Materials

Encyclopaedia Brittanica, 1911 edition

Statistics

Adoption Orders and Children adopted in England and Wales 1927–2011
Divorce Statistics in England and Wales, 1858–1971

Live births in England and Wales 1838–2010 within and outside marriage, and gender of child

The above are all sourced from the Office for National Statistics: www.statistics.gov.uk

Trade Directories

Gore's Directory for Liverpool and Birkenhead, 1900
Kellys Directory for Sheffield, 1881

Secondary Sources

Ashby, Robert: *The History of TACT (The Actors' Children's Trust)* (The Actors' Children's Trust, London, 3rd Edition, March 2013).

Behlmer, George K: *Friends of the Family: The English Home and Its Guardians, 1850–1940* (Stanford University Press, California, 1998).

Campbell, Nicky: *Blue Eyed Son: The Story of an Adoption* (Macmillan, London, 2012).

Cox, Pamela: *Gender, Justice and Welfare: Bad Girls in Britain, 1900–1950* (Palgrave Macmillan, London, 2002).

Cooter, Roger: *In the Name of the Child: Health and Welfare 1880–1940* (Routledge, London, 1992).

Cunningham, Hugh: *The Invention of Childhood* (BBC Books, London, 2006).

Davies, Hunter: *Relative Strangers: A History Of Adoption And A Tale Of Triplets* (Sphere, London, 2003).

Elliott, Sue: *Love Child: A Memoir of Adoption, Reunion, Loss and Love* (Vermillion, London, 2005).

Ellison, Mary: *The Adopted Child* (Littlehampton Book Services Ltd, Worthing 2nd Impression, 1958).

Grey, Daniel: '"More Ignorant And Stupid Than Wilfully Cruel": Homicide Trials And "Baby Farming" in England and Wales in the Wake of the Children Act 1908'. In *Crimes and Misdemeanours*, 3/2 (SOLON, Plymouth, 2009), pp. 60–77.

Fisher, Lettice: *Twenty-One Years, 1918–1939: A History for the Council for the Unmarried Mother and Her Child* (National Council for the Unmarried Mother and her Child, London, 1939).

Hardy, Sheila: *A 1950s Mother: Bringing up Baby in the 1950s* (The History Press, Stroud, 2013).

Hendrick, Harry: *Child Welfare: England 1872–1989* (Routledge, London, 2011).

Hendrick, Harry: *Children, Childhood and English Society, 1880–1990* (Cambridge University Press, Cambridge, 1997).

Higginbotham, A: 'Respectable Sinners: Salvation Army Rescue Work With Unmarried Mothers, 1884–1914'. In *Religion in the Lives of Englishwomen 1760–1930*, edited by Gail Malmgreen (Croom Helm, London, 1986), pp. 216–33.

Holmes, Jerry and Holmes, Jeremy: *John Bowlby and Attachment Theory* (Routledge, London, 2nd Edition, 2014).

FURTHER READING

Howe, David and Feast, Julia: *Adoption Search and Reunion: The Long Term Experience of Adopted Adults* (The Children's Society, 2000).

Keating, Jenny: 'Struggle For Identity: Issues Underlying The Enactment of the 1926 Adoption of Children Act'. In *The University of Sussex Journal of Contemporary History*, 3 (Sussex, 2001), online at www.sussex.ac.uk/history/research/usjch/pastissues.

Keating, Jenny: *A Child for Keeps: The History of Adoption in England, 1918–45* (Palgrave Macmillan, London, 2005).

Kiernan, Kathleen, Land, Hilary, and Lewis, Jane; *Lone Motherhood in Twentieth Century Britain: From Footnote to Front Page* (The Clarendon Press, 1998).

Knight, Lynn: *Lemon Sherbert and Dolly Blue: The Story of an Accidental Family* (Atlantic Books, London, 2011).

Kornitzer, Margaret: *A Baby is Adopted: The Children's Society Adoption Book* (Church of England Children's Society, London, 1950).

Kornitzer, Margaret: *Child Adoption in the Modern World* (Putnam, London, 1952).

Limbrick, Gudrun Jane: *How to Research Childhoods Spent in Former Children's Homes, Orphanages, Cottage Homes, and Other Children's Institutions* (Wordworks, Westfield Indiana, 2013).

Mason, Michael: *The Making of Victorian Sexuality* (Oxford University Press, London, New Edition, 1995).

Naish, Ethel M: *Whose Children Are These?* (Cornish Brothers, Birmingham, 1912)

Nicholson, Jill: *Mother and Baby Homes* (Allen and Unwin, London, 1968).

Nicholson, Virginia: *Singled Out: How Two Million Women Survived Without Men After the First World War* (Penguin, London, 2008).

Novy, Marianne: *Imagining Adoption: Essays on Literature and Culture* (University of Michigan Press, Michigan, Revised Edition 2004).

Novy, Marianne: *Reading Adoption: Family and Difference in Fiction and Drama* (University of Michigan Press, Michigan, 2007).

Payn, Graham and Morley, Sheridan: *The Noel Coward Diaries* (Weidenfeld and Nicholson, London, 1982).

Pinchbeck, Ivy and Hewitt, Margaret: *Children in English Society: From the Nineteenth Century to the Children Act, 1948* (Routledge and Kegan Paul, London, 1973).

Rattle, Alison and Vale, Allison: *The Woman who Murdered Babies for Money: the Story of Amelia Dyer* (Andre Deutsch, London, 2011).

Rose, Lionel: *The Erosion of Childhood: Childhood in Britain 1860–1918* (Routledge, London, 1991).

Ross, Ellen: *Love and Toil: Motherhood in Outcast London, 1870–1918* (Oxford University Press, Oxford, 1993).

Walker, Pamela: *Pulling the Devil's Kingdom Down: the Salvation Army in Victorian England* (University of California Press, Berkeley, USA, 2001)

Walker, Pamela: 'Adoption and Victorian Culture'. In *History of the Family*, 11 (Taylor and Francis, London, 2006), 211–21.

Winterson, Jeanette: *Why Be Happy When You Could Be Normal?* (Vintage Books, London, 2012).

Websites

This is a short list of online resources that researchers may find useful. You may also wish to consult the websites in the research section above, which are not repeated here.

www.actionforchildren.org.uk | www.theirhistory.co.uk
The website for Action For Children, the new name for National Children's Homes and Orphanage.

www.familysearch.org
This is a free-to-access and search website operated by the Church of Jesus Christ of Latter Day Saints. It is very useful for extracts from registers of places of worship of all denominations.

www.ukbirth-adoptionregister.com
Birth relatives and adopted people can register an interest in making contact with each other on this website, for a small one-off fee. This website is not the same as the contact register operated by the General Register Office.

www.victorianweb.org
For Victorian history, this is an excellent and wide-ranging website.

www.workhouses.org.uk
This is an outstanding website which has exhaustive coverage of the history of workhouses and poor relief in general. It includes pages on baby farms, boarding out and other child-related topics.

www. ancestry.co.uk | www. findmypast.co.uk | www.genesreunited.co.uk
These are examples of subscription websites that can be used for searching family history sources (no endorsement is implied by inclusion in this list). The websites are also useful for networking with individuals who have mutual research interests.

Websites for Specific Organisations
The following are particularly good examples, but there are many others on the Internet which are easily found using a search engine such as Google:

www.childrenscottagehomes.org.uk
This is an expansive website which aims to record the history of many of the cottage homes, children's homes and orphanages in England and Wales.

www.hiddenlives.org.uk
This is a superb website for the history of Waifs and Strays, with much archival material including case notes for a variety of children who passed through its care.

www.motherandbabyhomes.com
This is a website centred around an oral history project on this subject, with some excellent introductory articles giving a good context for the topic.

Glossary

Adoption Order
This is the document issued by a court at the end of adoption proceedings, which confirms and finalises the details of the adoption. It grants parental authority to the adoptive parent/s and in doing so, removes that authority from everyone else, including the birth parents and local authorities.

Affiliation Order
Another name for this is Bastardy Order. A document issued by a Quarter Sessions Court, Petty Sessions Court or Magistrates Court instructing a father to pay for a child's upkeep. In other words, the father becomes legally associated with the child and this association becomes a matter of record. Failure to pay could result in a prison sentence.

Asylum
Usually thought of nowadays as applying only to mental health institutions where those with mental health issues, and those who were thought to be morally defective (such as unmarried mothers especially up to 1959) were placed by the authorities or family. However, it was a word also used in the names of institutions which offered relief and support to the needy, such as orphanages.

Bastardy Order
(See Affiliation Order, above.)

Board of Guardians
From 1834, the administrative body authorised to exercise the Poor Law.

Eugenics
A belief in, and the practice of, a policy which used selective breeding (that is, choosing which adults could have children) to improve the human 'stock' and restrict those who would not, through their offspring, 'improve' that stock.

GLOSSARY

Mass Observation
A project begun in 1937 as a research organisation. A panel of observers and volunteer writers studied the everyday life of Britain. The work was especially useful to the authorities during the 1939–45 war. It continued in its original form until 1950.

Overseers
The officials who administered the local workings of the Poor Law on an everyday basis. This included escorting paupers from one parish to another after a removal order had been issued – some of whom would have been pregnant, unmarried women.

Poor Relief
The system whereby paupers and others who were not able to look after or sustain themselves were supported financially or in kind. This may include providing accommodation in a workhouse or other funded institution.

Quarter Sessions
A local court which met four times a year, presided over by Justices of the Peace. It was the court which dealt with bastardy, settlement and removal cases. More serious cases such as murder would be dealt with by Assize Courts.

Workhouse
A publicly funded institution into which very poor, less abled, and homeless people were placed by the authorities. In operation from 1834, known for its harsh system which dehumanised the inmates and acted as a deterrent to entry. Officially abolished in 1948. Similar but usually smaller institutions pre-date these workhouses.

Index